FROM THE ASHES

ALSO BY SHAUNTAY GRANT

The Bridge

FROM THE ASHES

SIX SOLO PLAYS

EDITED BY

SHAUNTAY GRANT

PLAYWRIGHTS CANADA PRESS
TORONTO

First edition: June 2023
Printed and bound in Canada by Imprimerie Gauvin, Gatineau

Jacket art and design by Leeya Rose Jackson of Noisemakers Creative Studio

Playwrights Canada Press
202-269 Richmond St. W., Toronto, ON M5V 1X1
416.703.0013 | info@playwrightscanada.com | www.playwrightscanada.com

LIBRARY AND ARCHIVES CANADA CATALOGUING IN PUBLICATION
Title: From the ashes : six solo plays / edited by Shauntay Grant.
Other titles: From the ashes (2023)
Names: Grant, Shauntay, editor.
Identifiers: Canadiana (print) 20230226906 | Canadiana (ebook) 20230227104 | ISBN 9780369104465 (softcover) | ISBN 9780369104472 (PDF) | ISBN 9780369104489 (EPUB)
Subjects: LCSH: Canadian drama—Women authors. | LCSH: Canadian drama—Black authors. | LCSH: Canadian drama—21st century. | CSH: Canadian drama (English)—Women authors. | CSH: Canadian drama (English)—Black authors | CSH: Canadian drama (English)—21st century
Classification: LCC PS8309.W6 F76 2023 | DDC C812/.60809287—dc23

Playwrights Canada Press operates on land which is the ancestral home of the Anishinaabe Nations (Ojibwe / Chippewa, Odawa, Potawatomi, Algonquin, Saulteaux, Nipissing, and Mississauga), the Wendat, and the members of the Haudenosaunee Confederacy (Mohawk, Oneida, Onondaga, Cayuga, Seneca, and Tuscarora), as well as Metis and Inuit peoples. It always was and always will be Indigenous land.

We acknowledge the financial support of the Canada Council for the Arts, the Ontario Arts Council (OAC), Ontario Creates, and the Government of Canada for our publishing activities.

To Jessica Care Moore, whose "Black Statue Of Liberty" called me to centre stage. And to Anne-Marie Woods, who encouraged me to stay there.

CONTENTS

Editor's Preface by Shauntay Grant | xi

Georgeena by Djanet Sears | 1

benu by d'bi.young anitafrika | 15

A Chitenge Story by Makambe K Simamba | 73

The Emancipation of Ms. Lovely by Ngozi Paul | 107

The Sender by Cheryl Foggo | 169

Crybaby by Kalale Dalton-Lutale | 183

Acknowledgements | 213

About the Contributors | 215

EDITOR'S PREFACE

BY SHAUNTAY GRANT

About fifteen years ago I was a student in an actor training program at a Canadian theatre. One of our classes focused on movement through body motions without speech—in other words, mime. Our instructor was a veteran in pantomime. Her style of teaching came with sweeping gestures and big expressions, her face routinely morphing between comic satire and dramatic calm. On this particular day she explained that, one by one, we were to stand on a figurative stage at the centre of the room and think private thoughts while slowly spinning around full circle. It was somewhat of an exercise in embodiment, since everyone had to guess who the student-actor had become in that particular moment (without the student expressly giving it away with words or gestures). "Someone on their deathbed?" "A student flunking out of college?" "A child?" Strangely, our guesses were almost always right. So when it came my turn I was confident my peers would empathize with what I was feeling, what I was offering from the stage.

I remember standing in that small, boxy studio—giant mirrors wall-to-wall. I looked straight ahead but fixed my eyes downward, trying to dodge my reflection in the glass. I stepped left to begin a slow three-sixty turn—not a sound except the scuffing of my shoes against the floor. I abandoned the idea of dreaming and instead settled into my own reality. I was not an elder or a student or a child; I was myself: a young woman peaceably fixed on meditating, tired in the way students are always tired, bolder with each step, longing for life, stories, culture, art . . .

"Oh yes, can you see it?" the instructor said, interrupting the end of my turn. All the students looked wonderingly at me. "Can you see it?" she asked again, pointing in my direction. "She's like the Black woman on the auction block; I can hear them now: 'She got good teeth!?'" She's hunched forward, fingers tapping away at her incisors. "'She got good teeth!?'" she says again, and I don't wait for a response. I walk off and sit down, pull my knees up, and lower my head.

I can feel my eyes moisten. "Oh, did that offend you?" I hear her say. I blink away a tear and look up, convinced I must be dreaming, searching her face and trying to rationalize this moment, to understand why my turn had been reduced to a haphazard "slave narrative" told in someone else's tongue. "Did that offend you?" she asks again, this time with her eyes. Everyone is watching me, wondering if I will answer. I look away, waiting for the room to move on. When it doesn't, I gather my knees again and fold back into myself. A classmate reaches for me, and I fight the urge to cry.

The impulse to edit a collection of solo plays by Black wom♥n began with this—an experience that halted any hopes I might have had for acting professionally. I finished the acting program, but I only went to one audition afterwards, my thoughts frequently drifting back to my movement instructor tapping her teeth and inspecting me with squinty eyes. In a city where Black theatre was—and still is—the exception and not the norm, I wondered what white directors saw when they looked at me. If they balked at my suggestion they consider me—a Black woman—for roles traditionally earmarked for white actors.

Some part of me had become unsettled at centre stage. And so my decision to prioritize playwriting over acting came in part from a desire to reframe the narrative that clouded my student experience; to tell my story, and stories from my community, on my own terms. But I would be remiss if I did not also acknowledge the many poets and playwrights whose work and words have influenced my writing for the stage. From Beah Richards ("A Black Woman Speaks . . . of White Womanhood, of White Supremacy, of Peace," 1951) to Ntozake Shange (*for colored girls who have considered suicide / when the rainbow is enuf*, 1976), Djanet Sears (*Afrika Solo*, 1987), and Jessica Care Moore ("Black Statue of Liberty", 1995), I have been inspired—by these and so many other literary luminaries—to write, discover, and champion Black wom♥n in theatre and performance. While *From the Ashes* does not represent the entire canon of solo plays written by Black wom♥n in Canada, it does offer a glimpse of what I feel are some of the most exciting offerings to emerge in this area over the past decade. With works that are autobiographical (or semi-autobiographical) and written for one performer, the plays in this anthology explore themes of Blackness, wom♥nhood, motherhood, mythology, racism, sexuality, and trauma, and champion Black wom♥n's bodies, stories, and experiences at centre stage.

Makambe K Simamba's *A Chitenge Story* follows a young woman who travels to her native Zambia to find and confront the man who abused her as a child. Based on her own experiences, Simamba bravely turns a tale of personal trauma into one of healing. Using the *chitenge*—a colourful African fabric—as a metaphor for memory, she roots her audiences in the sights, songs, language, and customs of Zambian culture in this gripping story that hits all the right notes and achieves a satisfying balance between seriousness and humour. In *The Sender* by Cheryl Foggo, a woman working for a global racism-elimination project encounters some technical difficulties when someone unexpectedly objects to the project's restrictions. Foggo skilfully uses an Afrofuturist methodology to unpack issues of race and racism, inviting us to consider parameters—both real and imagined—imposed on marginalized groups now and in the future. Ngozi Paul's *The Emancipation of Ms. Lovely* chronicles a woman's life as seen through different stages of her sexual awakening. Lovely's experiences are set against the story of Sara Baartman—an African woman who was exhibited as a freak-show attraction under the name Hottentot Venus in nineteenth-century Europe. Historic and contemporary representations of—and attitudes toward—Black women and Black female bodies converge in this multi-layered work that carries both tragic and comedic notes. And in *Georgeena* by Djanet Sears, a bride speeds down the highway, struggling to make sense of what led her to that moment, all while calming her emotions as she processes feelings of loss, anger, deception, and distress. Inspired by true events, Sears has created a character in Georgeena that is compelling, relatable, and wonderfully bold.

Other works in this anthology appear to blur the lines between playwriting and poetry. In Kalale Dalton-Lutale's *Crybaby*, a young woman falls in love for the first time, which opens a well of questions about her identity. Crybaby's adolescent years are unpacked through a set of linked vignettes—musings, aphorisms, poems—that effortlessly transport us back to childhood, amplifying a unique coming-of-age experience that rings familiar with its references to Barbie, *Anne of Green Gables*, compact discs, and classic breakfast food. And in *benu* by d'bi.young anitafrika, a young woman faces motherhood while still coming to terms with her own motherlessness. This second work in the sankofa trilogy is a thrilling biomyth that follows sekesu sankofa as shx enters into motherhood while confronting difficult childhood memories; her daughter benu is named for the mythical Egyptian bird—a predecessor of the Greek phoenix. Formally inventive, the play's scenes move through structural shifts—from conversations among characters that read like narrative prose poems, to poetic monologues and entire scenes conveyed by way of a line or two from a song. Like other works in this anthology, *benu* draws on the playwright's personal experiences, both lived and deeply felt, as witness to the worlds, histories, and stories that have surrounded them.

In her "NOTES OF A COLOURED GIRL: 32 SHORT REASONS WHY I WRITE FOR THE THEATRE" (in *Harlem Duet*, 1998), Sears equates writing with the experience of giving birth: "In a very deep way, I feel that I am in the process of giving birth to myself." In a similar way, the works in this collection can be interpreted as each playwright's creative offspring; through personal narrative and reflection as witnesses, they write themselves into existence. And like the ancient bird set ablaze rising from its own ashes, these plays collect the remnants of charred, challenging human experiences to shape them into well-formed works of art that cultivate connection, healing, hope, and love.

This book contains coarse language, racial slurs, and sexually explicit material including descriptions of sexual violence. Reader discretion is advised.

GEORGEENA
A TEN-MINUTE MONODRAMA

BY DJANET SEARS

PLAYWRIGHT'S NOTE

In the wake of the murders of George Floyd and Breonna Taylor, when race-based incidents are investigated in the media, it is common practice for journalists to examine the motivations of the perpetrators. We see it happening in the news today in reports about the US Capitol insurrection. We saw it when a Canadian "Karen," Amy Cooper, called the police on a birdwatcher in Central Park: "Why did (insert name of a Karen here) feel forced to attack (a description of a person of colour here)?" But do we know the name of the man she victimized? His last name was Cooper too—Christian Cooper. Another frequently asked question is "What is behind the rise in race-based attacks on people of colour?" Or "What drove (insert the name of a "Kevin"—a wannabe fascist—here) to want to be a Proud Boy?" If the injured party is Black, the news story will typically focus on the white attacker.

This short play was inspired by real events. It was also prompted by a two-decade-old study out of Duke University Medical Center by clinical psychologist Maya McNeilly, which suggested that "racist provocation" could lead to damaging physical and emotional symptoms. As McNeilly put it, "It is well-documented that racism has negative social, economic and political consequences on African Americans, but the direct effects of racism on physical and emotional health have only begun to be explored."

This story continues that exploration and contemplates the effects of the terrorism that overt and implicit white supremacy has on the physical and emotional life of one particular Black woman: Georgeena.

Georgeena aired on CBC Gem as Season 2, Episode 6 of Obsidian Theatre Company's *21 Black Futures* series, from February 19, 2021, to February 18, 2022, with the following cast and creative team:

Georgeena: Virgilia Griffith

Director: Weyni Mengesha
Set and Costume Design: Rachel Forbes
Lighting Design: Shawn Henry
Cinematography: Keenan Lynch

CHARACTERS

Geena Darsan

Canada Day. Late Night. Highway 400, Ontario.

GEENA *Darsan, thirty-seven, grips the steering wheel hard. She is silent. The drone of the car engine envelops* GEENA *and drowns out the faint bursts of fireworks on the horizon that intermittently perforate the night sky, lighting up the darkness.*

The phone rings.

She refuses to look in the direction of the singing phone and makes every effort to keep her gaze on the roadway ahead. She hardly blinks. She stares ahead of her, almost imperceptibly shaking her head, as if her brain is replaying a scene she does not wish to revisit. The faint sound of GEENA*'s heart beating begins to form a rhythm section to the constant drone of vehicular white noise and the ringing phone. The tempo of her heartbeat gets faster.*

A flash of neon arteries and veins radiating from deep inside her appear and disappear.

Beads of sweat form on her face. She glances over at the centre console, reaches to turn up the A/C, *and loses control of the vehicle for a millisecond. She quickly makes the correction. The phone stops ringing. The sound of her heartbeat begins to fade.*

GEENA *pulls off her recently acquired Vivica Fox bob, and the wig cap underneath, and tosses them onto the back seat. They land on the small pile of sparklers and handheld Canadian flags beside her designer overnight bag.*

GEENA's shoulder-length locks fall all around her. She removes several strands covering her face.

She reaches behind her back, and with some difficulty, unhooks her bra. She slips an arm through the bra straps one at a time under her top. She flings the bra onto the back seat. With one hand still on the wheel, she wrestles to peel herself out of her girdle. She manages to get the tight-fitting foundation garment down to the top of her hips, then gives up the losing battle.

She removes a high-heeled sandal from her left foot. She places the now bare foot on the accelerator and removes the other shoe from her driving foot. She throws the shoes onto the passenger-side floor.

The sound of her phone ringing again pierces the white noise.

GEENA's jaw tightens. Her heart beats faster again. The faint network of neon arteries and veins become apparent, but for longer this time. They pulse to the polyrhythmic beat created by her heartbeat and the ringing phone.

She takes a deep breath, glances over at her trembling purse on the passenger seat beside her. Then, making every effort to keep her eyes on the road, GEENA carefully reaches for her purse. It's beyond her grasp. She trains her eyes on the yellow line in front of her, unlocks her seat belt, extends her arm, and leans towards the adjacent seat. She locates the purse and slips her hand inside.

A light emanates from the soft leather tote, illuminating the darkness. She retrieves the phone and the ringing stops abruptly.

She sets the phone on her lap. She dials, only glancing down from time to time to ensure she's pressed the correct button. The dialled number begins to ring.

MATHIEW: *(off stage)* This is Mathiew Spruyce. Obviously I can't get to the phone right now. So please leave a message, or send me an email to mathiewspruyce@mailbox.ca. That's M.A.T.H.I.E.W.S.P.R.U.Y.C.E. at mailbox dot—

She presses End. The car has begun to veer out of its lane. She quickly adjusts the steering.

GEENA *leans in the direction of the passenger seat, rummages inside her purse, takes out a single-sided earphone, and places it in her ear.*

She pulls her seat belt over her chest but has trouble locking it with one hand.

The phone rings. She abandons the seat belt and presses the Bluetooth option on the phone in her lap.

GEENA: No, no, no. No— No, no . . . I am not a cockroach! Cockroaches do not drink wine from long stem glasses. Cockroaches cannot tell the difference between a zinfandel and a shiraz. Cockroaches don't earn PhDs and run their own labs at the university. Even if she believed— We were eating. We were having dinner and she— No, don't you dare, don't you dare— I don't care that she used to be a zoologist. That research is so goddamn old. First, cockroaches did not come to the new world with Africans on slave ships. Second— Sec— That, that, that scholarship is blatantly wrong. Fossilized cockroaches have been carbon-dated in Europe, Asia, Australia, and the Americas. They are forty-four to forty-nine million years old. So the notion that cockroaches accompanied my, my tortured and abducted ancestors like some, some kind of invited guest.

The network of arteries and veins slowly reappear, and can be seen through her clothes and skin and flesh. A blister appears on the surface of her chest, near her neck.

And I even checked. Afterwards I checked. 'Cause this kind of accusation . . . this kind of shit always makes you think it's you. For a second I thought I must have made it up— No, I was the cockroach in your mother's analogy. You were the cockroach. All Black people were the cockroach.

GEENA *touches the blister with her finger. The area is tender.*

I do not care that she adopted you when you were a baby. I don't care that she loves you. I don't care that I was the first Black woman you'd ever brought home! I don't care about the goddamn dress. I don't care that 153 friends of ours, and family members, will descend on your family's home tomorrow. I don't. I was, I was sitting at your family's magnificent ivory-and-blackwood dining table, the day before my wedding, defending whether the lives of Black people goddamn matter, for god's—

The network of arteries disappears, leaving only the wound on her chest.

Of course all lives matter. You know that. Why can't they hear the implied "too" when it comes to Black lives? Black lives matter . . . too! Black lives matter too— And that's a problem. That's a very big problem. That's why you said absolutely nothing. How the hell can you understand were she's coming from— He had skittles and ice tea in his pocket, for Christ's sake, Mathiew. We went to the march during the lockdown. I thought . . . You could've, you should've, you didn't have my back— Telling, telling your mother that there are two sides to every . . . That is not having my back! There are not two sides. Okay, no, no . . . there *are* two sides. The right side and the goddamn wrong one. Your mother is so— We're talking about, we were discussing the execution of a twelve-year-old human child. Jesus Chri— She was accusing me of not being open to discussing . . . how is . . . how is cutting off oxygen to a human being the appropriate punishment for selling cigarettes without a license? Why is this even a discussion— She's hurt? What— I did not call her a racist. 'Cause god forbid you call a racist a racist. Negotiating the right *of Black people to live is okay.* But calling— When your father said he doesn't see colour, did I say anything. Did I? No. I was a good ole Negro. So what exactly does he see when he looks at me? You are your father's Black son. Adopted Black son. Does he see you as white? And I want you to know that it took everything, everything in me not to slap your brother. "Take Canada Back"? You have a white brother who's going to vote for a Reform conservative putz that wants to "Take Canada Back"? Take it back from who? And his gallerina wife posing with that Make America Great Again hat. That hat is not a joke. And that's supposed to be funny? He thinks it's funny? And I'm dying inside. And you laugh.

GEENA *tries pulls her seat belt on again.*

You're laughing with him like a good little Negro.

Her skirt appears to be covering the seat belt buckle holder.

Then I defend myself and suddenly your mother's all hurt, and suddenly it's all about her tears.

She lets the seat belt buckle go.

She calls me a cockroach and it's my fault she's crying. I did not call her a racist. 'Cause we all know that calling any of them racist would be worse than Sandra losing her life, or Breonna being murdered just 'cause the police barged into the wrong house. Ha. White tears, Black lives—

Her reaction to what she's saying makes her lose control of the vehicle. She makes a quick recovery.

Don't you dare, no. I've always . . . I've always been that, that proud Negro, that cultured Negro who uses her intellect to convince people like that to, to see . . . see me . . . Everything I do. Everything I've done is about convincing them . . . I'm human. I'm human too. But when she . . . at best she was blaming Black people for cockroaches. At worst she was admitting that's how she saw us. And I don't care that she's worked on herself, worked on her biases. She thinks of me as a cockroach. Your intelligent cockroach girlfriend. Your charming cockroach wife-to-be. And it just came out—

The network of arteries inside her body are visible again.

Yes— Yes, I did. I told your mother, "Fuck you." I told your father, "Fuck you." I told your brother and his wife, "Fuck you"— The wine glass was in my hand. I'll pay to get the stains removed. (I will pay) because I should've known better. It's better to sit there sipping shiraz, negotiating with you, with your mother, about whether white people have the right to take my life—that it's better for me just to sit quietly and try to understand why they think white people have a right to kill me. And it happens every day. Usually they're more subtle. More *insidious* . . . like paper cuts. Most Black people average thirteen race-based paper cuts a day.

Welts emerge from the intersection of blood vessels and skin.

Sometimes more. That's over forty-seven hundred race-based cuts a year. Nearly fifty thousand cuts a decade. Most scab over quickly and heal. Some ooze at first. The psyche tries to push out the toxins, and the skin has to bind the exit wounds. And paper cuts hurt in a way that other cuts don't. It's the nerve endings. There are so many nerve endings on the skin, on the hands, fingers. It's more painful. They hurt even after they heal. Some never heal at all. And then there's the terror of it. The terror of wounds yet to come. Will the salesperson . . . Will the doctor . . . I live with that terror every fucking day.

Even more welts begin to appear.

My psyche is a galaxy of scars. My soul is a burn victim. And when you get scarred, your skin gets tight, thin, brittle, inflexible. Touch me the wrong way at times, too harshly, without consideration, and I will crack and my insides will seep out. I will not live like that—

The welts erupt.

Don't you dare . . . I tried. I always try. I've worn my best Vivica Fox wig to every family event. I have a PhD, yet every time I see your family, I have to spend so much time on my goddamn makeup—

GEENA *is now covered in barely visible scars.*

I'm not blaming you, Mathiew. I'm blaming me. What am I doing watching makeup tutorials? I've replayed one video so many times I can recite it by heart. I am contoured to the FUCKING gods. My cheekbones . . . The bridge of my nose looks so sculpted, so thin, you'd think I was Meryl Streep playing Nina Simone. And of course a pinky-blush lipstick, not the deep browns I love. You hate the browns. I know you hate the browns—you kiss me more when I'm not wearing browns? I'm not blaming you. But . . . I don't know. I don't know. I'm tired. I'm tired of smiling in the face of this shit. It's not what I want for my life. Not my personal, my intimate life. I don't want to hide my hair when I leave my house. I don't want to disguise the bridge of my nose. I no longer want to hide the umber, brown, ebony, black of me just for people to treat me— To see me as more like them. More human. To see me not as a cockroach—

GEENA *sees the eruptions. She sees the scars. She gently rubs the affected areas.*

I'll call them first thing— Yep. I'll send out a, a mass email or something when I get— Just call the pastor. If guests show up—

Her eyes become a river.

Yes— Yep— Can you call the pastor—

A stream delicately carves its way down her cheek and onto her lips.

Okay— 'kay— Uh-huh.

Her weeping becomes sobs. This is not a pretty cry. It is full of brackish water, snot and spit. She struggles to hold the steering wheel.

She takes several deep breaths.

Do not confuse my tears with regret. I was crying . . . I am crying because . . . I love you, you know. I'm just crying because—

Flashing lights and a siren interrupt her.

Shit! Gotta go.

GEENA touches the phone.

MATHIEW: *(off stage)* What? Geena?! Geena?!!!

GEENA ends the call and allows the phone to slip from her lap onto the floor.

She steers the car to the shoulder of the highway. The flashing lights and sirens follow her.

She begins to reach into the back seat for her wig, but thinks better of it.

She puts both hands on the steering wheel in such a way that it's clear she has nothing in them. She notices the seat belt dangling beside her.

GEENA: Oh shit!

She nervously takes the seat belt and buckles it. Her heart begins to beat loudly. Her arteries become vivid and clear. The network of blood vessels shudders and shakes.

She goes to grab the steering wheel again, but thinks better of it and places her hands in the air.

The sound of her heart beating is deafening. A bright, flashing light shines on her through the driver's side window.

Whiteout.

benu
the sankofa trilogy, part II

by d'bi.young anitafrika

for my brothxr johari stewart
there were three of us
now there are two

for you amaka
mothxr* of khaleel
sometimes wi ban wi belly and wi bawl

for you, mentor
I am forever grateful for that moment in which you mothxred me

* I consciously "x" gendered pronouns like "womxn" and "mothxr" to challenge colonial gender norms embedded in english. this promotes an inclusive understanding of gender, acknowledging those identifying beyond the binary. the "x" adds a queer element to gender, which questions how language enforces gender binaries. it's meant to disrupt these norms and make readers actively question binary genderfication. the "x" is an invitation to explore the expansive spectrum of gender identities.

production hxrstory

benu (workshop) was presented at la chapelle theatre as part of their 2009–2010 season in tiohtià:ke,* kébec,† from february 6–14, 2010, with the following company:

playwright/storyteller: d'bi.young anitafrika
director/dramaturge: natasha mytnowych
lighting design: kimberly purtell
original music: waleed abdulhamid and laurence stevenson

other productions of benu

la chapelle, tiohtià:ke, 2010
tarragon theatre (*the sankofa trilogy*), tkaron:to,‡ 2011
aki studio (*the sankofa trilogy*), tkaron:to, 2014

---

* the island of montreal has long-standing connections to the haudenosaunee and anishinaabeg indigenous peoples. the island is recognized in the kanien'kéha language as kawenote teiontiakon, a hxstorically documented name. additionally, the city of montreal is referred to as tiohtià:ke in kanien'kéha, and in the anishinaabemowin language it's called mooniyang.

† "kébec" is an algonquin word that refers to the province of quebec.

‡ "tkaron:to" is the wendat and kanien'kéha word that is the origin for the name of the city of toronto.

development hxrstory

benu (workshop), an original commission from la chapelle theatre in tiohtià:ke, kébec, was first presented as a workshop production at the havana theatre at the sisterhood celebration festival on the unceded territories of the musqueam, squamish, and tsleil-waututh peoples* in march 2009.

playwright/storyteller: d'bi.young anitafrika

~

benu (workshop) was next presented at anitafrika! dub theatre as part of the audre lorde workshop festival in tkaron:to, ontarí:io,† in may 2009.

playwright/storyteller: d'bi.young anitafrika

~

benu (workshop) was next presented at theatre passe muraille (mainspace) as part of the summerworks theatre festival with anitafrika! dub theatre in tkaron:to, ontarí:io, in august 2009 with the following company:

playwright/storyteller: d'bi.young anitafrika
director/dramaturge: natasha mytnowych
lighting design: kimberly purtell
original music: tova kardonne and waleed abdulhamid
stage manager: paul beauchamp

* "vancouver, british columbia," is located on territory that was never ceded or given up to the british monarchy by the musqueam, squamish, or tsleil-waututh peoples.

† "ontarí:io" is a wendat word meaning "great lake" or "beautiful water" from which "ontario" derives its name.

~

benu (workshop) was next presented at the registry theatre as part of the impact 09 theatre festival by mt space and anitafrika! dub theatre on the traditional territories of the anishinaabeg, haudenosaunee, and neutral peoples,* ontarí:io, in september 2009 with the following company:

playwright/storyteller: d'bi.young anitafrika
director/dramaturge: natasha mytnowych
lighting design: kimberly purtell
original music: waleed abdulhamid and laurence stevenson
stage manager: paul beauchamp

* "kitchener" is located on the traditional territories of the anishinaabeg, haudenosaunee, and neutral peoples.

synopsis

sekesu sankofa, daughtxr of mudgu sankofa, is a new mothxr entangled in a web of unexplained headaches as shx tries to make sense of hxr life post-delivery. shx is led down a path of fear, discovery, and renewal—like the phoenix that rises from its ashes—in a tkaron:to hospital. reality meets myth, magic meets ritual, as the second story in d'bi.young's biomyth monodrama trilogy unfolds in firesome ways.

element

the magical story of the benu bird

setting

bird-womxn
atop a willow tree before time

baby
benu sankofa in various settings as shx is on hxr way to being born

an emergency room
a hospital in tkaron:to

mothxr mudgu
in accompong, maroon mountain village, xaymaca*

* "xaymaca" is the taíno indigenous people's name for the island renamed "jamaica" during spanish and english colonization.

props

a chair

three white bird feathers

a white fabric (representing the phoenix's skin, the baby, the baby blanket, and a bedsheet)

costumes

a hospital gown

music

a balafon / a violin

characters

sekesu sankofa
young womxn striving to survive new mothxrhood (age in brackets)

mudgu sankofa
sekesu's mothxr

bird-womxn
a being who is part mudgu, part sekesu, part bird

granny
sekesu's grandmothxr (mudgu's mothxr)

pearl johnson
mudgu's best friend, sekesu's neighbour

paul
sekesu's partner

nurse patrick
sekesu's nurse

clerk
a secretary at the hospital emergency room

anaesthesiologist
indifferent to sekesu's experience

dr. obrien
a passerby in the hospital

dr. shand
sekesu's nigerian doctor, tells sekesu about hxr positive pregnancy test

prosecutor
reads benu's charge in court

pre-show
bird-womxn

stage is flooded by light
a violin chirps like the tones of a blood-pressure machine in the distance
a chair sits centre stage
three white eagle feathers are scattered close to the chair
a bird-womxn is stooped atop the chair
covered by the white of hxr unfolding
shx breathes silently yet visibly
hxr body expanding and contracting with exhales and inhales
shx is content

scene 1
bird-womxn

the bird-womxn sits atop hxr tree
nesting an egg of myrrh that contains hxr mothxr's ashes
as the lights begin to transition so does the bird-womxn
the balafon and violin serenade changes
a clashing cacophony begins
the egg begins to rumble
birth, death, rebirth
the bird-womxn is determined to leave hxr cocooned state
of egg nesting, the egg determined to do the same
shx moves rhythmically in the chair
illuminating different body parts
head, arms, elbows, knees, face, pressing hxrself up against hxr fabric skin
birth, death, rebirth
the lights fade slowly
the music does not
and the bird-womxn is never uncovered

scene 2
baby benu

black
clashing balafon and violin
pierced by sekesu's voice
they end abruptly
sekesu is centre stage
in agony from labour contractions
shx is nine months and two weeks pregnant
shx addresses hxr grandmothxr

sekesu (28)
pressure! more! more pressure! pleeeaaaaasssse you have to press harder! not there! right here! press! please press!

sekesu pauses, breathes heavily

no I don't want an epidural! I don't want that thing in my back, granny! granny! you never told me it was going to be like this granny you never told me it was going to be no epidural.

(to granny) can't they just take it out, granny? eeeh?

overwhelmed with contraction

presssuurreeeee! pressure! pressure! pressure! you have to press harder please!

shx snaps at a nurse

I said I don't want an epidural.

the contraction passes

granny? granny please tell them to take it out of me granny I want them to take it out now granny! granny I feel as if I'm going to die, am I going to die? granny am I? I'm going to die? I don't want to die like this! granny I don't want to die! pressure! pressure! I want my mommy!

another contraction hits

pressure! pressure! pressure! . . .

stage goes dark

scene 3
emergency room

sekesu in er waiting room
talking to womxn with baby
to the right of hxr

sekesu (29)
wow is the er ever packed up tonight. what kind of baby is it?

shx looks longingly at the baby in the womxn's arms

you know my great-grandmoddah shx had one daughtxr. then my grandmoddah shx had one daughtxr. then my mothxr had one daughtxr, and then I have one.

shx winces in pain and holds hxr head down

it doesn't matter what kind. they are all children, children . . .

shx remembers childhood with granny

that's what my granny used to say, after I had the baby shx decided to go back to xaymaca, you know shx was living here for over twenty years, said shx couldn't stand the cold anymore, so when shx go back to xaymaca, shx going to open up a store just like the one we had up on eglinton west. up there we used to have a shop for all these years, where my grandmoddah used to sell bread and eggs and fish and rice and flour and all kinds of little knixknax like those. people on eglinton used to buy up the goods so fast. granny always had to go to the wholesalers to restock the goods in the shop.

shx never sold tamarind balls there though. no tamarind balls. no candy. no sweety. but whenever shx went to the wholesalers shx would bring back tamarind balls for me.

(to audience members) so where are you from?

voice of audience member
the islands.

sekesu
the islands, which one of them.

voice of audience member
saint kitts.

sekesu
saint kitts, I'm from xaymaca. well I was born in xaymaca but very soon after I was born, my grandmoddah was living here in kanata,* shx came down and got me, one foot in xaymaca, one foot in kanata.

(to audience member) in saint kitts, do you have to call the people who are older than you aunty or uncle? or ya can call them by their first name?

voice of audience member
aunty and uncle.

sekesu
same ting here! you would swear that my grandmoddah were raising me in xaymaca. every one of the people who are older than me I have to call them aunty and uncle, including that womxn who used to live in our apartment complex *(exaggerated)* miss pearl. I had to call hxr aunty pearl, even though I know shx never liked me. you know my grandmoddah whenever shx went to the wholesalers, shx would bring tamarind balls for all of the children in our apartment complex and they all had to call hxr granny even though really shx was only my grandmoddah.

---

* "kanata" is a wendat word meaning "village" or "settlement," which possibly influenced the settler colony name "canada."

hxr head hurts

ooohhh my head again.

shx looks up

that's why I'm here. I've been getting these headaches. they feel as if they are getting worse. no family doctor, emerge is the next best thing.

shx takes a deep breath

there, it's passing.

shx looks around at all the people in the er

wow is it ever packed in here. I hope I see somebody soon . . .

so where you from? . . . ahhhhh . . . so you know back home you couldn't call somebody older than you by their first name right . . . it had to be granny, auntie, uncle, blood or no blood. but I didn't do that all the time, especially with pearl.

shx corrects hxrself, laughing

I mean auntie pearl. shx could chat chat people business you see, and always have an opinion 'bout whatever is going on, especially when it come to the children in the yard.

granny would come home and give all a we one tamarind ball each, covered in brown sugah and salt. I always imagined some big, black, round, womxn in coronation marketplace who smelled like a combination of honey and dirt, plopping down hxrself on an old piece of log and having a mound of tamarind balls, picked fresh from the tamarind tree, sitting right in front of hxr. to the left, a tub of brown sugah. to the right, a smaller container of salt. then shx press lightly on the outer shell of the pod, and it fall away, open, between hxr fingers, exposing the brown, gooey pods inside. shx remove each pod and dip them one by one in sugah. then sprinkle a likkle salt. then roll them roll them in sugah again. did you know you can get three to four tamarind balls from one tamarind stalk? . . . yes.

my granny didn't sell tamarind balls in hxr shop though. no sweety, no candy, nothing like that. but shx didn't mind bringing it from market for us. we would play ring games and wait for hxr to come home.

shx launches into a children's hand game

twee twee twee
and away we go
nelly belly swelly
shx cyaan tell hxr mommy
di faddah is a mystery
hxm come from cincinnati
whe shx a guh do
shx disobey di rule
shx too fool fool
shoulda stay inna school

pearl johnson
you sekesu, you don't have anything bettah to do than to sing about slackness, baby, and bxyfriend? you think those things are fun and games for you to be playing brown gxrl in di ring with. not everything is a joke, sekesu. you never get any homework to do today? you are the likkle fire starter of everything, eeeh?

sucks hxr teeth and cuts hxr eye at sekesu

sekesu
ms pearl . . . never really liked me. but shx lived in our tenement yard so I couldn't avoid hxr. granny always come to the rescue though and walk through the gate just in time. all of us would run up to hxr and hug hxr up and laugh and search hxr up for the tamarind balls dem. hmhmhm.

shx basks in the memory

and after that, story time . . .

scene 4
bird-womxn

balafon and violin paint a magical picture
as the bird-womxn performs a ritual dance
around the chair, preparing hxr nest for incubation
granny becomes the bird-womxn
shx speaks in a deep, thick, rich jamaican accent
sitting atop hxr tree on the rocking chair
the skin-fabric becomes the egg the bird-womxn sits on

granny
children, children, do you know how likkle ones like you come into being? once upon a time a very long long long time ago when everything was black and still a willow tree wept "*please bird-womxn lay your egg.*" there was a winged-womxn who dwelled upon hxr ben-ben stone, high atop the very last branch of a willow tree. enveloped by the womb of blackness, nesting an egg of myrrh that contained hxr mothxr's ashes. this womxn, hxr egg, the ben-ben stone, and the willow tree was all that ever was. sometimes, the bird-womxn felt the vibrations of the willow as it wept. the willow was lonely. but bird-womxn knew it was not time. when the willow wept, the bird-womxn took pause from hxr sitting and kissed white-eagle-feather-soothing unto the willow's drooping trestles. until the next time the willow's tears fell . . .

scene 5
emergency room

sekesu in er waiting room

sekesu (29)
you know that story, that was one of my favourite stories of granny . . . if I helped granny on saturdays with the market bags, I could get hxr to tell me that one. plus I would get something extra special—another tamarind ball . . .

scene 6
sekesu in institution

sekesu (30)
I wonder if I could get tamarind balls in this place
where is this place? how long have I been in this place?
benu? benu sankofa!?
my daughtxr benu,
where are you? where are you?
at night birds fly
swooping up and down and into water
gorging mouths drenched pungent
I am the catch of the day
while silver tuned circles beckon
the sun outstretched
smiling at dawn
I am an enigma
benu, benu, "*I am cutting you in two*"
you said, you said, "I cut you in two and *put a river in*"
I cut you in two and wash you clean,
wash you clean
I cut you in two and wash you clean,
wash you open
benu I am still open,
benu my child I am still open
and I miss you
I miss you

scene 7
emergency room

sekesu in the er waiting room
shx is hesitant and distrustful

sekesu (29)
I'm having a crazy time . . .

shx realizes how long ago

a year ago now. what a turning point. I had a birth journey and a half—yes! twelve-hour labour, epidural, c-section, inflamed liver, high blood pressure, low blood pressure, racing heart, fainting spells, head pressure, eye pressure and ear pressure shortness of breath, low oxygen . . . then irregular beat, head pressure, ear pressure, eye pressure, can't focus, can't drive,

shx screams

can't think!

remembers where shx is

and now more headaches . . .

scene 8
baby benu

sekesu with baby in arms
prepping to leave the hospital after delivery, shx converses with nurse patrick

sekesu (28)
you all really made the past two days fantastic for me and the baby, nurse patrick, just one more day to go and then it's home sweet home.

shx does a little dance

no more hospital food, no offence nurse patrick but the hospital food *(side eye)* no. but I can't wait . . . oh baby, oh yeah the baby's crib's been ready for a while. I mean really we waited and waited for ms. latey-pants to decide when to exit the comforts of the womb . . . *(kisses teeth)* eight days late nurse patrick . . . and you know I knew that shx wasn't going to come through my vagina . . . shx was huge, ten pounds. there was no way shx was gonna pass through these hips and I knew it. and I told them just give me the c-section right away but noooo.

anesthesiologist
(patronizingly) miss sankofa we here at the hospital, we are experimenting with a new smaller epidural needle and we really believe that with this new smaller needle complications arising from epidurals will certainly diminish, if not completely disappear. certainly diminish considerably, to the degree where you the patient will feel little to no pain at all before and long after you take said new smaller epidural. what do you think miss sankofa?

sekesu
what do I think . . . ? how can somebody get all that info when they're in sooo much pain. of course they're gonna agree to anything. so I said yeah, gimme de epidural and then five hours later still no baby. I ended up having the c after all nurse patrick. I can't believe that.

looking at hxr baby

but that's all yesterday's news, ey baby? now it's home sweet home.

(to nurse patrick) oh yeah, the headaches are coming, they're going, not so bad today. yeah I feel pretty good. the headache's subsided. you know nurse patrick, I had a bowel movement this morning . . . the pills you gave me, they worked . . . yeah my milk is pretty much in. I think too much actually.

scene 9
sekesu in institution

sekesu (30)
my milk-filled breasts, my childless breasts, my breasts like mountains marooned on the slopes of my potential for being. my benu-less breasts.

shx looks intently at the walls

these walls, these walls look like fire today, these four walls, these imprisoning walls, these walls hot in their containment and angry at their man-dated stillness. these walls want to tumble, crumble, and run white in the streets like concrete lava, paving all, saving nothing. a retribution of sorts for being caged birds, muted, mutilated, they want to break out bust out bust a move. dance on the heads of the ones who claim to know but don't know everything.

these walls like irokos in an ancient enchanted forest. stoic and magical. these walls know truth, rooted for decades observing the lonely ones uprooted, we are uprooted who wish we were walls ourselves. walls who could not be punctured, pumped, pimped, pilled, patronized. these walls do not need parents, lovers, partners to survive. walls who stand with a permanent no! no! no! unrelenting, I don't want an epidural unyielding, I don't want an epidural unforgiving. I don't want an epidural. no!

sobbing as shx returns to hxr seat

scene 10
emergency room

sekesu (29)
I live just by the shopping centre at square one which means that I can go there whenever I need anything! like, furniture to match these wicked pink curtains that I saw on sale last week. ohmigod . . . what's wrong with pink? . . . nothing's wrong with pink. you should see my curtains. they are soooo bright. I'm sure they'll help cure me of the winter blues. every year it's the same thing, no sun, no shine. brighter curtains, that's the way to go. I'm telling you.

shx glances at the er

I swear that man came after I did and hx's going in. I have never known er to move this slow. this is slower than back home. and then once you're past triage, they park you up for hours . . . I know. it's a trick to keep you passive so you don't mind waiting longer, on the inside.

shx laughs

granny was good to go back home. shx was living here a long time ago, then when I was born in xaymaca, shx came back to help take care of me . . . ahhh.

shx holds hxr head

. . . this thing just won't stop . . . my granny raised me in a tenement yard in wid one chattabox pearl johnson who I always had to call auntie pearl cuz shx was older than me.

scene 11
bird-womxn

balafon and violin revisit bird-womxn serenade
the bird-womxn performs a ritual dance
around the chair, once again preparing hxr nest for incubation sitting
atop hxr tree on the rocking chair
the skin-fabric becomes the egg the bird-womxn sits on

granny/bird-womxn
children, children, this bird-womxn sat up on hxr ben-ben stone, nesting hxr egg of myrrh that contained hxr mothxr's ashes. hxr wings folded into themselves many times over. when they were open, these wings spanned the circumference of time itself, and so, shx kept them folded as shx pondered the willow's request. the bird-womxn sat. children it is said that this bird-womxn had the beak of a cock, the face of a swallow, the neck of a snake, the back of a tortoise, the hindquarters of a stag, and the tail of a fish, and children, white eagle feathers for wings. these wings children were the wings of the breast of a goose.

granny pauses and thinks for a moment.

and wings covered in white eagle feathers. yes children. these magical wings were the ones she would flap when flying, when fanning the flames of creation for the time for the little ones, the little ones, the little ones like you to come, children. with when time came. it was the only way to make passage for the little people, like you, to come.

scene 12
baby benu

sekesu is leaving the hospital
hxr friends sandra and patricia have come to pick hxr up

sekesu (28)
oh, sandra, patricia, you guys I'm so glad you came to pick us up from the hospital, oh little baby your two crazy aunties are here, yeah everything's packed and ready to go . . . well what did you bring me? shx's so cute, oh my god! . . . look at hxr nose . . . I know shx has my nose. it runs in the family. thanx for coming to get us girls . . . I don't know what I would do without you two . . .

what did you bring me? you brought me the water of a boiled coconut shell. why? better if you brought me some coconut water but I'm not complaining . . . and what else did you bring me? mint, thyme . . . what is this red string for? tie around hxr hand. why? . . . protect hxr from what?

shx laughs

shx laughs, then notices hxr friend about to light an incense stick

you can't light incense in the hospital room . . . because it will set off the fire alarm. not to mention them coming to see what kind of afrikan voodoo black magic simi-dimi going on round here.

shx laughs again

benu

. . . baby, you see your two *eccentric* aunties, we call them the witches! no, sandra I did not wash out the house. when did I have time to wash out the house? you know that I had a c-section, I've been in here for days . . . good when you go home you wash out the house, alright . . . anyways let me just go and say bye to nurse patrick and then we can go.

nurse patrick
gxrl don't say to hx say or shx say, listen . . . don't tell them that I said anything you know, they give you an epidural gxrl . . . I think they does be causing your headaches. you should have never taken that thing. that thing will drive you stark raving mad gxrl. gxrl between we, don't say that I say to hx say or shx say cuz next thing you know they saying I losing my job because I telling the truth, but every womxn who they does give that thing does end up sooner or later in some madhouse you hear me.

it does give yuh headache, then yuh feel faintish, then yuh in anoddah reality all together. you see what I mean.

don't tell them that I say, but I believe they does be running experiment gxrl. yes . . . as soon as you can you go and get a wash out and a bathe down. gxrl, you does know 'bout shango baptist? shango baptist! where you does come from? . . . xaymaca, well, good enough. I hear they does have obeah people over there? is not no shango baptist but it will do. so you make sure you find yourself a good obeah womxn. god only knows what kind of thing put inside that thing! and remember you never hear it from nurse patrick.

sekesu stands, shocked by what shx has heard

scene 13
sekesu in institution

sekesu (30)
silhouettes
benu I am longing to know you benu
I can't know you
benu like drowning the weight of this love resuscitates me
our beings are too light and grace for this place

scene 14
baby benu

sekesu dances happily singing to the baby

sekesu (28)
(singing) carry mi ackee guh a linstead market not a quarty wut sell
carry mi ackee guh a linstead market not a quarty wut sell

oh lawd what a night, what a plight, what a satiday night
lawd what a night, what a plight, what a satiday night

everybody jusa feelup feelup whe dem mumma nuh bring everybody jusa feelup feelup whe dem mumma nuh bring oh lawd what a night

what a plight
what a satiday night
lawd what a night, what a plight, what a satiday night

awww benu, you and mommy are finally home, look at you, your nose is so cute you know I know that is your fxther's nose
what a satiday night

scene 15
baby benu

sekesu (28)
yeah . . . yeah I'd have a baby with you. well because you're cute . . . I'm cute, why not. I think the baby would look real nice, are your friends having children? no, my friends aren't having children. I guess because they don't want to interrupt their careers, or maybe they don't want to be burdened. or maybe they live with their parents and that cannot gwaan . . . you know, bringing baby-belly inside their parents' house . . . no I don't live with my parents, so that's not a cause for concern . . . yeah I used to live with my grandmoddah but shx went back home. too cold. and it was time for me to get my own apartment. older than you. what about my mom? . . . no I wasn't raised by hxr . . . because I just wasn't . . . I wasn't alright . . . can you stop with the twenty questions, you're killing the vibe.

sekesu passes out momentarily

scene 16
bird-womxn

balafon and violin revisit bird-womxn serenade
bird-womxn performs a ritual dance around the chair, shx mounts the egg
the egg begins to rumble
it is time

granny/bird-womxn
and then children the egg began to rumble. it rumbled and rumbled beneath hxr. at first shx thought this rumbling to be the willow tree's. but slowly, as hxr entire self was taken over by an overwhelming shake, shx realized that it was time. to go. carefully shx unfolded hxr wings and spread them. then shx lifted hxr body off the egg and enveloped it in hxr hindquarters. the willow smiled. it knew what was about to happen. the bird-womxn at once flew over the waters of possibility; hxr magical white wings casting a mighty shadow on the entire earth. this deep shadow created an uproar of waters that made them bubble with potential, forever changed, children.

scene 17
baby benu

sekesu (28)
what just happened to me? what do you mean I passed out? no I'm fine, I'm fine, baby it's okay don't worry. how long was I passed out for? . . . yeah I got a bit of a headache but I feel fine. I said I feel fine . . . baby I'm okay *(changing the subject)* so what did you do to me while I was passed out eh . . . yeah right you needed more time.

shx laughs

what would it be like to have a baby? yeah I know it's a lot of work but I mean if our parents didn't have babies we wouldn't be here. you gotta see it like an investment in your future . . .

paul is taken aback

yeah. children could take care of you when you're old. I'm not going to no nursing home. the odds are in my favour. I'll have one or two or three; one of them will take care of me when I can't take care of myself.

I didn't say I wanted to have it with you paul, so you can stop worryin' . . . really? you would have a baby with me?

shx says doubtfully

really? you're just joking . . . don't play around with stuff like that . . . next ting you know you call down baby-spirit on both of us and we haven't even gotten tested . . . you love to take risk with your life . . . you don't even know if I am crazy . . . crazy.

scene 18
sekesu in institution

bird/sekesu
benu
benu I'm coming
I'm coming benu
mommy would never leave you benu
benu
benu
cry
cry when love's labour loses hxrself in a sea of habitual passions
flames scorching like the sun
breaking the bands of redemption that you and your lover pledged by the riverside,
cry
where do I get to bask in branches of brighter days
my sap supple sweet
my beacon beckoning and knowing
in you, benu, in you I return to the sea of unending sunshine,

wandering nomad herded warrior
I smell the silenced tongues of time towering breathing brown
into the one the all-knowing one

I wish I knew the pulsating palms of beyond rooted, reaching into the soil's past plates shifting vibrating a smiling change that must come, and you will still be there

benu

where do I bask in branches of better days
holding steadfast to sap sapple sweet
my beacon dark and bright and grey
in you, benu, in your return to the womb of unending sunshine

scene 19
baby benu

sekesu in doctor's office for routine checkup

dr. shand
sekesu sankofa, sekesu sankofa. we didn't see anything on the cat scans. I'm not sure what is causing those headaches. I think I'll send you for some further testing. oh yes . . . one of your tests did come back positive . . . you are pregnant.

sekesu stands staring into space as the news that shx is pregnant sinks in

sekesu in er waiting room

scene 20
emergency room

sekesu (29)

talking with er visitor

the er makes me nervous sometimes but I guess it's the fastest way to find things out.

shx laughs

no, no family doctor, I figured I would come tonight, you know because it's quicker. you go to a family doctor then you have to wait to get the requisition forms, then you have to take your requisition forms to the examination centre, then you have to do the test, then you have to wait and I mean, so much time could pass in that time, you could.

(to audience member) something could happen to you right? er, er is the best way, none of my friends are having children, I don't know why they all wanna wait until they have their careers together or they don't want to be burdened or they live with their parents and that just can't gwaan. well when I found out I was pregnant I went right to the shopping centre and I bought a stroller and I bought baby bottles, I bought diapers, I bought everything. I keep getting these headaches. I live by the shopping centre at square one. I can go there whenever I need anything like, say, baby clothes!

with a coy, excited look in hxr eyes

none of my friends have children. they're all waiting, not sure for what. I bought a stroller, and a change table, and diapers, and bottles and . . . sooo many things . . .

scene 21
baby benu

sekesu at hxr apartment with paul

paul
woaw. ahhhhhh . . . that's not exactly the news I was waiting to hear . . . wasn't really expecting that, that was what you were going to tell me when you said you had a surprise for me, ya know I thought maybe we were going on like a movie night or something you know, I mean this baby thing . . . that's a bit heavy because we're still young teenagers you know I mean . . . what about school I'm not even done school and and and I want to see the world . . . well, how can that be . . . we used a condom always . . . except that one time . . . I mean it was one time . . . I for sure pulled out before anything happened . . . I can't do this . . . not right now . . . I've got law school to finish, and and and I've gotta see the world . . . and and and what about my parents . . .

sekesu (28)
what about your parents? . . . what about your parents . . .

shx stares at paul intently

. . . what . . . am I not good enough or something for them?

paul
listen man I didn't say anything about being good enough, all I'm saying is that my parents have expectations of me ya'know, I'm not a statistic. ya know I'm not just some black man who ups and has a child then walks out on their child's life, like I have plans ya'know? like, I was planning to have a family and raise my family ya'know? and be there, but this? this I can't be there . . .

sekesu
what do you mean you can't be there . . . when we were talking everything was fine everything was fine, paul, this baby inside of me? this is our baby. we can do this, I know this is spontaneous I know this is soon, but paul we can do this, please. okay, if you need a little bit more time, you can think about it.

paul
think about it? I don't have anything to think about, well I'm thinking that thing inside of you is growing what about womxn's lib . . . are you ready to be burdened by a kid. what about feminism and womxn's right to choose to abort . . . they've got plans for me sekesu. I have plans . . . I'm not ready . . . are you sure?

hx hesitates

that it's mine. I mean you do have other lovers, don't you? . . . I'm just saying . . . if I am not the only one you were sleeping with, then it could be somebody else's right?

sekesu
. . . ion it's not gonna happen, it's never gonna happen, my mothxr had me at fifteen, granny says at fifteen shx shx was fine, fine fine, and I'm almost thirty . . . and I'm stronger and I'm wiser. it's not the same situation, it's different, yeah you're 50 percent of this, it's terminal, but it's my right to choose, and I choose to be a mothxr. hey, I want to be a mothxr, benu, hey I did want to be a mothxr benu, I did I did . . .

disappointed by hxs lack of excitement but maintaining hxr own

this baby is ours. and I want it. if you want to wait until it's born to have a paternity test to settle the question then let's do that . . . I want you. and I want us. and I am afraid too. and I am happy. and impulsive and pregnant . . .

hx does not respond

well, if and when you are ready. let me know. until then. no regrets.

paul
no regrets? for you maybe. for me, this is the biggest mistake I made of my entire life. I'm not even twenty-five yet. I want a real family that I can be there to take care of, when I'm ready. I'm not another black man who just ups and leaves hxs child. I'm not a statistic. you say that this baby is ours. but you are making all of the decisions without any consideration for my feelings. I'm 50 percent of what you have inside of you right now and yet you are being so selfish. I mean you are an educated womxn, what about womxn's lib . . . are you ready to be burdened by a kid. what about feminism and womxn's right to choose abort—

sekesu
don't even go there. don't even go there. my mothxr didn't go there and shx was fifteen and poor and shx was fine, shx did fine fine fine fine fine. and yeah, they might have taken me away from hxr, but that wasn't hxr fault. it wasn't hxr fault.

shx spirals momentarily

I'm older, stronger, my body is stronger, more ready.

back to paul

it's not gonna happen. it's not gonna happen you hear me? you hear me? yeah you are 50 percent alright, sperm and all, but this is my body. and my *womxn's right* to choose what I want to do with it, including parenting . . .

scene 22
sekesu in institution

sekesu dances to hxrself, rocking back and forth

sekesu (30)
lawd what a night what a plight what a satiday night
lawd what a night what a plight what a satiday night

scene 23
bird-womxn

balafon and violin revisit bird-womxn serenade
granny continues hxr story

granny
the bird-womxn, children, and so the bird-womxn flew and flew and flew. hxr wings casting a mighty shadow upon the world below, uproaring the waters of possibilities, hxr wings creating the animals and the plants and the people, and all life. and what of the little ones to come, for the little ones to come children, the bird-womxn needed to fly to the sun, to the sun shx flew.

sekesu in the emergency room

sekesu (28)
hx won! hx actually won! I seen it in my time. I can't believe it. black president. that man can tell a story you know.
as a child I was mesmerized by the possibilities—watching my grandmoddah weave hxr web of stories like a quilt. my grandmoddah. mothxr of my mothxr.

scene 24
sekesu in institution

sekesu (30)

collecting the feather-white cloth to form a baby bump

my mothxr mudgu, hxr fifteen-year-old legs stretch and tear and refuse to bend, braced by an unwavering resistance. hxr legs my mouth, hxr screams my blood whispers. darkness before time. legs that do not bend in resistance to a life of labels. hard life like barbed wire fence. stiff and unforgiving. I am of my mothxr, beckoned.

if I squeeze my inside part I keep you inside me benu. here there are no mirrors of phallic encounters.

or enchanted nightmares
spanning deserts
of broken vessels
or unsanctioned travel
or talking sticks now beating sticks
turned measuring sticks and sticks and stones breaking my bones

I am of my mothxr. my mothxr. a calling. my mothxr's fifteen-year-old legs like toppled stilts waving possibilities. upturned and high and determined and fifteen. my mothxr.

searching for mothxr

mommy, mommy

my mothxr of who I am?

scene 25
bird-womxn

balafon and violin revisit bird-womxn serenade
granny tells the children the bird-womxn story

granny
the bird-womxn, children, flew and flew and flew. as shx did so, hxr shadow met the embrace of the wind, transforming the water below into mountains and valleys, land, rivers, animals and things. in hxr flight the world was created. but what of the little ones? for that the bird-womxn needed to arrive at hxr final destination. do you know where that was? no? that was the sun. to the sun shx flew and flew and flew and flew, still carrying hxr egg of myrrh containing hxr mothxr's . . .

scene 26
emergency room

sekesu (29)
you know last night I had a dream . . . dream last night 'bout a game named piss on the people politricks. the objective, stand up on the tallest building and gather as many people as possible below. pull out your penis and piss and piss and piss. far far far wide wide wide. and the man on the tallest building who pisses the furthest is the prime winner . . . I had a dream last night about this gated condominium community. a funeral procession of benz, bmw, jaguar, and lexus driving through the sky-high, great-wall-of-china-long fence celebrating the death of my rights? my mothxrly rights, my womxnly rights, my humxn rights? black womxn, people of colour, first nations peoples, disabled people like animals on a farm in the year 1984.

shx begins to walk around the chair

caged in bantuland reservations.

hxr eyes dart back and forth as if shx has figured something out

each subdivision armed with an electric chair for public execution. I had a dream last nite that some doctor, some psychiatrist, some psychologists, some psycho psycho psycho psychist . . . psychists . . . hysterics, hysterical was playing a game with my life.

some time passes

it hasn't stopped. the headaches are getting worse. I can't concentrate. listen I'm trying to explain to you, just listen please it's not in my head, it's not in my head. when I feel my heart skip a beat, it's not in my head. when I feel like I am going to faint it's not in my head. okay okay you you think that I might be experiencing some kind of unknown soon-to-be discovered kind of panic attack, one where your heart skips a beat, your adrenalin releases, you feel faintish but all you're doing is sitting down.

I say if you come to the hospital emergency room and you're not dying then nobody will see you. at least not soon enough to prevent you from dying. my head is killing me. I mean I called ahead and told them I was coming so long ago. and now hours have passed.

clerk
ma'am you have to fill out a form just like everyone else . . . yes yes yes . . . well you should have filled out the form when you got here. yes you still need to fill out that form ma'am. just fill out that form and put it in the grey bin and wait over there.

sekesu
fill out a form, I have to fill out a form but I told them I was coming and I came here hours ago and now I have to fill out a fucking form.

dr. obrien
(with british accent) excuse me ma'am, you are in a hospital emergency room. you cannot be screaming at the top of your voice. if you are displeased with the service here, then there are many more gta emergency rooms to visit.

sekesu
what? many emergency rooms in the gta for me to visit. but I called ahead and told them that I needed to see a doctor and I just need to see a doctor cuz my head is killing me . . . I was told to fill out a form and wait, even though I have already been here for hours. my head is fucking killing me.

some more time passes

sekesu (28, 29, 30)
I mean okay, I'm not saying that I would do what that womxn who jumped off the 401 did okay, I'm not saying I would throw my child over the 401 and then jump, ok that's not what I'm saying! all I'm saying is, this weekend I rented a car to help me and the baby get around, because you know taking the

bus with the baby is so hard, you've got the stroller and nobody wants to help you and they all look at you, like "look at that young black gxrl, oh another statistic, oh shx must be a welfare mama," so you know it's hard to take the bus, so I thought okay the best thing to do is rent a car. so I rented the car right, and I was trying to get everything into the car and so. I put the blue bag into the car, and usually I leave the car seat for last but because of this.

holds head in agony.

I put the car seat into the car, and then suddenly the doors close and I realize, I'm not in the car . . . I started banging on the window, bang bang bang. and I think "oh my god if the glass shatters it could cut the baby," no no let me get the spare keys. and I ran into the house but I can't get into the house because the house keys are on the car keys and now everything's in the car except me. and look the phone is in the car too so then I think okay, let me go to the neighbour, I go to the neighbour.

(to neighbour) neighbour? neighbour? can you help me please? oh thank god you have one of those jaws of life things, and we go to the car and we open the door and I grab the baby. but my head, my head is going . . . boom . . . and boom . . . and boom . . . and I mean I could never do what that womxn did on . . . the 401 so instead I flew, and flew, and I flew and I flew and I flew . . .

sekesu experiences a severe panic attack . . .

sekesu's memory enfolds hxr

bird-womxn
shx flew and flew and flew and flew and flew and flew and flew.

sekesu (28)
pressure! harder! harder please!

shx desperately whispers to hxr mothxr

granny tell them to take it out of me granny. I don't want to die granny. I don't want to die.

sekesu descends even further, hxr voice is manic

benu

I went to the doctor last week and I felt like I was pregnant. my bxyfriend wasn't too happy about it. I figure if you are having sex, you must know that pregnancy is a possibility. and I want to be a mothxr. I want to be a mothxr.

granny
and flew and flew and flew and flew and flew and flew . . .

sekesu
(at the ultrasound) if something was wrong with the baby I would feel it right? cuz we are connected. if something was wrong with me I would know it right?

shx sees the image of the baby on the ultrasound

that's the baby's feet. and arms. look look look oh my god it's the face . . . no no no I don't want to know the gender. I want to be surprised . . . oh I love surprises. my granny used to give me surprises all the time.

bird-womxn
and flew and flew and flew and flew and flew and flew . . .

sekesu (29)
benu, benu mommy's head is hurting you have to stop crying baby, baby please just stop crying, I need to see the doctor, I need to see the doctor, benu stop crying . . . look at this place. I clean it again and again and again.

(to the baby) stop crying. you are always crying. my head is killing me.

(to hxrself) I just need to see the doctor, but I can't leave the baby like that. stop crying.

scene 27
baby benu

sekesu (28, 29, 30)
benu don't cry. dry your eyes, mama will sing you a lullaby . . .
benu don't cry. dry your eyes, mama will sing you a lullaby . . .

shx thinks about what lullaby to sing . . .

groovy here I am cum rub it pon mi belly like a guava jelly
damsel here I stand cum rub it pon mi belly like a guava jelly

benu I'm sorry, I'm sorry baby, I'm sorry for shouting, mommy didn't mean to shout at you. it's just that mommy is having a very difficult time right now. don't worry baby, mommy will never leave you. I'd never leave you like my mothxr left me. but it wasn't hxr fault, granny says that shx was too young to have me, fifteen. that something, something happened, shx won't tell me what happened, but they sent hxr, sent hxr away, they sent hxr away in xaymaca. granny, granny said that it was the best thing to do, that was the best thing to do.

I would never leave you, I would never leave my child, never, never not like my mothxr left me. it wasn't hxr fault, it wasn't hxr fault the world can get so lonely, it gets so lonely, baby okay mommy have a plan, alright, alright? what mommy is going to do. . . mommy is going to get this headache business taken care of once and for all, then it's just going to be you and me and you forever. you just sleep right now and mommy's going to go to the doctor and see someone who can help, and you just stay right there, don't move. don't move and mommy will be right back alright? I'm just going down the road to the hospital. I'm just going to the er, it move fast and mommy will be right back. don't move mommy loves you.

there was this chatterbox womxn in xaymaca, pearl johnson. shx never really like me. granny told me that pearl and my mothxr were the best of friends. they grew up together. granny say that pearl and mudgu used to walk the street with their nose running like river, and granny would have to wipe their noses and send them inside to put on shoes because they loved walking barefooted on the concrete. it's you and me now benu. I will always love you. and never leave you.

look at your nose. that's really your dad's nose you know. someday you will meet hxm. hx's soooo cute. you look just like hxm.

I love you benu sankofa. daughtxr of sekesu sankofa. daughtxr of mudgu sankofa. daughtxr of many daughtxrs of daughtxrs. don't cry.

I'm going now, to the hospital, to get this head business taken care of once and for all. you sleep, shhhhh sleep, benu. and before you wake up I will be back. I love you.

scene 28
emergency room

sekesu (28, 29, 30)
yes I am sekesu sankofa. is it time for me to see the doctor now, I've been here for so long . . . okay I'm coming with you. what why are you putting that on me . . . why are you putting those on me? where are we going? I want to see the doctor. my baby? my baby is just at home. no I didn't do anything to my baby, no please, please take these off me, where did you take hxr? I am what? arrest for what? wait wait wait . . . what are you guys doing? I didn't do anything to my baby . . . what are you talking about? . . . my baby is fine . . . please let go of me . . . where is shx? where is shx? what have you done with hxr? where is benu? let go of me! let go of me! . . . I want my baby! I want to see hxr now!

sekesu confused

benu, benu where are you? mommy's right here, mommy would never leave you, I want to see my baby! let go of me! I want to see my baby! I just need to see the doctor!

mommy is here baby. mommy won't leave you. mommy won't leave you ever again. never. never. never.

sekesu switches and begins to talk to hxr mothxr

mommy? mommy? mommy? mommy why did you leave me? why did you leave me? mommy mo . . . mo . . . ben . . . mu . . . mu . . . mu . . . I want ta . . . I want to see . . . it was my fault. it was me you left. if I wasn't born, shx wouldn't have left. mommy. I'm sorry. I'm sorry. I'm sorry.

benu

completely breaks down

it's all too much too much too much too much too much too much too much too much too much too much too much too much too much too much too.

scene 29
bird-womxn

balafon and violin revisit bird-womxn serenade
sekesu and granny play hide and seek

sekesu (7)
granny? granny? you found me granny you never seen me hiding behind this granny? granny? can I have one extra tamarind ball today? granny because it tastes so nice, and plus when you put it inside ya mouth granny you suck it up and then mmmmm you swallow it and then it's all gone granny, granny? can I please have another one.

sekesu leans forward to eat the tamarind ball

mmmmm, thank you granny. granny granny tonight you know which story I want to hear granny, I want to hear di one about that bird-womxn, remember the one where shx have that egg inna and shx just fly away and egg had something funny.

shx remembers

ashes, can you tell me that one pleeeeaaassse? . . .

sekesu's memory shifts

remember you said if I help you with the market bag, you would give me something really nice. . . I know I always have a tamarind ball but it's soooo sweet granny, and salt, and bitter. and it melts down into something soooo good and you suck it up and press it out with your tongue. by the time you swallow it's gone. sooo can I have another one pleeeeaaassse? . . .

shx opens hxr mouth for granny to place another tamarind on hxr tongue, which shx does.

granny which story you telling tonight? a duppy story!

shx turns to hxr cousins, who are all afraid of ghost stories.

well if you don't want to hear a ghost story then you should just go to your bed! I'm big and I am not afraid. please granny can we hear the one about ashes . . .

scene 30
bird-womxn

sekesu is on trial

prosecutor
all rise. the honourable judge crawford presiding. the crown vs. sekesu sankofa. on july . . . in the year . . . benu sankofa was found alone and crying at 137 crescent drive. the child was severely dehydrated and distressed. the child's mothxr sekesu sankofa could not be found. the child was removed and placed in the care of a family member. sekesu sankofa, you are charged with gross negligence and endangering the life of your child benu sankofa. how do you plead . . . ?

sekesu turns to face the audience, directly engaging them, the bird-womxn merges with/in hxr spirit
and ascends into the sun . . .

bird-womxn
I am the future of me. I am my past. I am the deep swelling of potential coming. I am water. I am breath. I am the crone. older than blood-bleeding wounds which never dry, for I am water. and with that, children, the bird-womxn flew. shx flew right into the sun. from the ashes emerged the little ones like you, you are free to choose your destiny. children children.

laughing

the continuation . . .

A CHITENGE STORY

BY MAKAMBE K SIMAMBA

for the Mwanang'umbi women

A NOTE ON THE CHITENGE

Chitenge, (pronounced CHI-TENG-GEH) is a Zambian word for the African fabric that coloured my childhood. In other African countries, chitenges may go by many other names, including *chitenje*, *kitenge*, *kanga*, *capulana*, and *ankara*.

Chitenges are often found wrapped around the hips of women for both casual occasions and a variety of ceremonies. They can also be found holding babies snugly to their mother's backs, or being fashioned into the most beautiful custom garments you've ever laid your eyes on.

To me, there is no better symbol of my Zambian culture than the chitenge, and this is not just because of its beautiful aesthetic. This colourful cotton fabric is also a powerful metaphor for memory, and the ways memories can soften, stain, and stretch. Sometimes memories tear, and sometimes, they wrap themselves around us and carry us to places we never expected.

A Chitenge Story was first produced by Handsome Alice Theatre in Calgary, Alberta, from March 20–24, 2018, with the following cast and creative team:

Playwright and Performer: Makambe K Simamba
Director and Lighting Design: Kathryn Smith
Sound Design: Aidan Lytton
Set and Costume Design: Sarah Uwadiae
Stage Manager: Kennedy Greene
Production Manager: Andrea Rocchio

A workshop presentation of *A Chitenge Story* premiered at Intrepid Theatre's UNO Fest in Victoria, British Columbia, on May 22, 2016, with the following cast and creative team:

Playwright and Performer: Makambe K Simamba
Director and Designer: Kathryn Smith

CHARACTERS

Makambe
Kuku
Niece
Cousin
Old Aunty
Young Aunty
Uncle
Villain

WELCOME HOME

Lights up.

A Movement Piece: KUKU *enters with a charming smile. She dances, showing the audience her chitenge, a beautiful piece of African fabric that she always wears. We see her in the vibrancy of her youth.* KUKU *exits.* MAKAMBE *(twenty-one) enters, puts down her jacket and suitcase and looks frantically around the room, then exits.* KUKU *enters again, and we see her body joyfully age into the greatest grandmotherhood. She transforms the space. She opens* MAKAMBE*'s suitcase.*

KUKU: *(speaking Silozi) Ka ka kuzize. Ka nahana kuti akana za ku bulela.*

She notices the audience.

Let me say it in your tongue. "She's a quiet one, that one. Thinks she doesn't have much to say."

KUKU *goes through* MAKAMBE*'s things, laying her clothes out on the floor.*

Is this a shirt? Or a dress?

She touches MAKAMBE*'s phone, and the music video for an obnoxious rap song starts to play.* KUKU *watches for a moment, and then tries to turn it off. She doesn't know how to work the touch screen. She drops it into the suitcase and then turns it off magically by gesturing with her hands.*

She finds a makeup bag.

I don't understand the young girls these days— Always painting their faces. Each time they leave the house, their lips are a different colour. I know it makes them feel nice, but I think they are beautiful as they are.

She smells the clothes and arranges them in a very particular pattern. She reads them. She puts a white tank top with lace on the clothesline.

She's a quiet one that one. Doesn't think she has much to say.

KUKU exits. MAKAMBE enters.

MAKAMBE: I've only been here two hours! Why does my family think it's okay to keep rifling through my stuff?

She starts to put her things away.

Oh yeah. It's because I'm in Zambia, and privacy is not a thing. I'm just saying, it would be nice not to have to share space with twelve other people, but, uh, I guess when you show up unannounced, beggars can't be choosers.

When I was a kid, it was always "Please Mummy, can we go to Aunty Monje's house, please please please pleeeease?"

Well, Aunty died six months ago, it's now her son, my cousin, who runs the house . . . and just to give you an idea of how well we get along, he now insists on calling me *Muzungu* girl . . . which means "white girl," so that's a thing. And there is this *kuku* here (a grandma), who hasn't said a word to me, but keeps following me around the house, not to speak to me, but just to stand in the corner . . . and smile . . . for long periods of time. Don't even get me started on all the other characters called relatives who live in this house.

She takes a deep breath to centre herself.

None of that matters because I am here on a mission. I only have five days, and I will not fail.

COUSIN enters with photo albums.

COUSIN: Good news, *Muzungu* girl! I found the photo albums you asked for. Ready to take a stroll down memory lane? The terrible two back together again.

He opens an album.

Let's start with the baby pictures. *Damn!* I was a CUTE baby—nice and fat, rosy cheeks, sunshine smile since age zero. Remember this?

Ha, matching outfits. Double denim. We should do it again!

He flips the page.

Oh, I remember this one! Mum found us in the cupboard and we were covered head to toe in flour. She was angry. Wasn't it even your idea?

MAKAMBE: I was uh, kind of hoping to do this on my own.

COUSIN: Oh. Oh. Okay.

COUSIN leaves.

MAKAMBE: Finally.

She holds the albums close and closes her eyes.

Please.

MAKAMBE scans through the photo albums frantically. She doesn't find what she's looking for. She throws the album aside and goes to bed.

THE VILLAIN'S HAND

A Movement Piece: While MAKAMBE *sleeps, the* VILLAIN*'s hand appears. It creeps up to her face. She shakes it off. It creeps down her arm. She shakes it off. It creeps down her leg.* NIECE *wakes her up.*

NIECE: Aunty Makambe! Wake up! Do hurry, do hurry!

MAKAMBE: Are you okay? What's wrong?

NIECE *leads a concerned* MAKAMBE *into the yard.*

NIECE: *(out of breath)* I want to play a game.

I want to play *waida*. I'm going to teach you, so that you can teach all your *Muzungu* friends in Canada. Because *waida* . . .

Sassy NIECE *puts her hand on her hip.*

It's a nice game, Aunty. That's why I'm going to show you *waida*.

NIECE *begins to set up for the game. She takes a rope traditionally made from the fibres of an old sack and ties it around two posts.*

You kind of remind me of Aunty Sikuka. She also used to live with *Muzungus*, but not Canadian *Muzungus*, England *Muzungus*. When she came to visit, she brought me two T-shirts, one jersey, one jeans, two socks, two shoes, and four chocolates.

(holding her hand out) You, what did you bring for me?

MAKAMBE: Myself.

NIECE: *(unimpressed)* I like your bracelet.

MAKAMBE gives NIECE her bracelet.

Okay, this is how you play *waida*, one of the games for *waida*. It's called *Demama*. Watch me *nicely*.

NIECE stands in the middle of the long oval created by the suspended rope. NIECE is enthusiastic, but terrible at the game. She sings as she moves her feet quickly in and out of the rope.

Demama de
Upside down
Demama debula
Upside down

Fish double fish double
Upside down
Fish double fish double
Upside down

Dina Mango
Kotapela
Dina Mango
Fya ku sashila

Your turn!

COUSIN: *(off-stage) Yela wena ka sizani!** I got a surprise for you.

NIECE: Sha!?† Yes, Uncle?

COUSIN enters.

* Hey there, little girl!

† Yes!?

COUSIN: There's Fanta . . .

NIECE: FANTA!?!?!?!!!

She exits, running.

MAKAMBE: Fanta.

Beat.

COUSIN: Do you like softies?

MAKAMBE: What?

COUSIN: You used to love them, Ms. *Muzungu* Canada. Softies? Soft drinks.

MAKAMBE: Oh, you mean like, pop.

COUSIN: *(imitating her accent) "Yeah, I mean like, pop."*

MAKAMBE: Stop calling me that. Here, I'm *Muzungu* girl, but at home, I'm a Black, and it feels like—

COUSIN: Oh, so Canada is home.

MAKAMBE: My point is, why can't I just be Makambe?

COUSIN: It's pronounced, *Makambe.*

Look, if you want the softies, help yourself. I bought twelve crates.

MAKAMBE: Why did you buy twelve crates?

COUSIN: Ah-ah. Because I'm a good person! Because we haven't seen you in sixteen years! Because I wanted to make you a party. I even bought talk time for fifty thousand Kwacha and called the entire family. But ever since you came, you don't socialize so the party doesn't make sense, so I called everyone again—more talk time, and I told them not to come. *Tst.* Come to think of it . . . you owe me talk time.

Beat.

MAKAMBE: A party?

COUSIN: Not anymore, *Muzungu*. Hence the softies.

MAKAMBE: You didn't have to cancel.

COUSIN: You want to have party?

MAKAMBE: Well, who's going to be there? Like, family?

COUSIN: Yes, of course family.

MAKAMBE: Extended family?

COUSIN: Yes, the whole family. Everyone we know was invited. You want to have a party?

MAKAMBE: Yeah. Let's have a party. Woo!

COUSIN: Okay, *Muzungu* girl. Party on! We'll do it tonight!

COUSIN excitedly sets up for the party. He exits.

A SOLDIER PREPARES

A Movement Piece: MAKAMBE *is in her room getting ready for the party. The sound of drumming fills the space, and she is in a trance.* MAKAMBE *navigates the stage like a soldier about to go into battle. She undresses, down to her underwear. She observes her body.*

MAKAMBE: People are starting to arrive.

He could be out there right now, driving through the gate and parking his car, or manning the braai, flipping the chicken over the coals . . . or maybe he's lying in the grass, playing with the kids and . . .

Beat.

I am READY for this.

She grabs her dress, holds it like a gun, and stalks her prey.

I just have to keep my cool and stay focused. When I find him and know it's him . . . I'm going to walk right up to him . . . look him straight in the eye . . . AND PUNCH HIM IN HIS STUPID FACE.

The trance ends.

A popular Congolese soukous party song starts to play. She enters the party, but stays at the edge of the room.

Cousin told everyone to be here at five . . . So people started arriving at eight. Who knew my family was so huge?

She looks around the stage for him.

There's food, laughter, dancing. Softies. Everyone is having such a good time except for me. I don't think I see him.

She cautiously enters the crowd.

There's an unfortunate irony in being at a huge party that's being thrown for you when you wish you could be invisible. People keep coming up to me, and I'm running out of ways to avoid them.

NIECE: Aunty Makambe! Hi! In school, we were learning about Canada last term. Me, I passed number one!

MAKAMBE: That's nice.

MAKAMBE tries to move away.

NIECE: Me, I know all of the province names in the whole of Canada. Do you want to hear? All of the province names?

MAKAMBE: You know what sweetie, I do want to hear, I really do. But Aunty is busy, so tell me another time. Go and play with the other kids, okay?

NIECE: *(circling around MAKAMBE)* OKAY! B is for British Columbia! A is for Alberta! S is for Sasisisikatechewan! M is for Manitoba!

OLD AUNTY: AH! Makambeeeeee! Praise Jesus, he granted the travelling mercies and brought you here safely for this delightful surprise visit. Last time I saw you, you were like thiiiiiiis.

She indicates a height that is very close to the ground.

Do you remember me?

MAKAMBE: *(lying)* Mhm.

OLD AUNTY: With the grace of our Heavenly Father, you are so tall now, almost a woman, going to university, you've even developed some little breasts.

MAKAMBE: Thank you for that. I have a question for you. Are these all the men in the family?

OLD AUNTY: You want to find a man? Mmh! I suppose it's about time, Makambe. You are what now? Twenty-one? But first, finish your studies. After that, we will be expecting a ring and a nice *lobola.** And then we hope you will be blessed with some little ones, in God's timing. Because God's timing is the best timing.

MAKAMBE: It sure is.

OLD AUNTY: The Bible says be fruitful and . . .

MAKAMBE: Multiply.

OLD AUNTY: My church has a nice pamphlet about this. It's lying around here somewhere.

MAKAMBE: No, Aunty. Wait.

OLD AUNTY: My plate? Yeah, you're right. Time for round two.

MAKAMBE: Are these all the men in our family?

OLD AUNTY: You can't find a man, here, Makambe. You're related to everyone. The Bible wouldn't like that. Speaking of men, let me go and make sure the grandpas didn't eat all the chicken, and I'm coming back to talk to you properly when I find that pamphlet.

MAKAMBE is terrified. OLD AUNTY exits just as we discover YOUNG AUNTY sitting on a chair.

YOUNG AUNTY: *Kono munani lika zende koo kwa Canada.* I said, you have nice things over there in Canada.

That is a *nice* belt, hm. The colour really compliments your skin tone.

* Bride price.

Us? We have nice things in Zambia, but not like that: the belt. Which is from Canada. If only I had a nice niece, to buy me stuff like this, that's nice . . . that they don't have in Zambia, but it's there, in Canada.

MAKAMBE: Aunty, would you like my belt?

YOUNG AUNTY: *(gasping)* For me? *Wow.* This is beautiful. *Kono** Makambe, you really know how to buy nice stuff you for your Aunty. I wasn't expecting this. *Bo*† Slyvia! Look what Makambe just brought me from Canada!

UNCLE pulls MAKAMBE aside and invites her to sit down.

UNCLE: Makambe! Come come come come here! We need to talk! Serious-serious stuff!

MAKAMBE: Please can we please talk later?

UNCLE: No. What type of jobs are there in Canada? Tell me the main industries currently stimulating the GDP. I'm very skilled, but you know this economy? The Kwacha has never been the same since President Chiluba. When it was Dr. KK . . . the grandfather of this nation, we were fat! Those were the good old days. Now, there is so much nepotism . . . you can't get anywhere unless you know someone!

MAKAMBE: Mmmhmm.

MAKAMBE gets up.

UNCLE: Are you listening? Pay attention!

MAKAMBE sits down.

What connections does your dad have in government? He should use his power and influence to help his own.

MAKAMBE: Isn't that nepotism?

* But.

† A gender-neutral title of respect.

UNCLE: Ah-ah. What's your point?

MAKAMBE: You're right. I'm going to call him.

(patting herself down) Oh my God, you know I left my cellphone in the next room. I'm going to grab it and call him immediately. You stay here.

MAKAMBE escapes into the pantry.

COUSIN: *Muzungu* girl! I see you! Why are you hiding in the pantry?

MAKAMBE: I just needed a moment.

COUSIN: I don't get you. You come home and surprise us, so I decide I want to make you a party. But when you arrive you don't want to talk to anyone, so the party doesn't make sense, so I cancel the party. I cancel the party, and then you tell me, "Why did you cancel the party?" so I make the party. I make the party, and now, you don't want to talk to anyone again, and you're hiding in the pantry talking to a bag of beans?

You think because you live with the *Muzungus* in Canada, you're better than us, but *this* used to be your home.

MAKAMBE: I'm not trying to be difficult.

COUSIN: You're not difficult. You're boring. We're having a party and you're in the pantry. Everyone came to see *you*. Everyone wants to talk to *you*. LOOSEN UP, *ah-ah*! You're STIFF like an ironing board.

MAKAMBE: I see you've had a couple to drink.

COUSIN: Duh. It ain't fun if it's only softies. What's your poison? What do you guys drink in Canada? Beer? No. Hard stuff, eh? Whiskey? Crown Royal?

MAKAMBE: People are still arriving, right?

COUSIN: Ohh, it's a mystery? You're a hard *Muzungu* to crack.

(singing) She doesn't like whiskey, and she doesn't like beer. Tequila? Not for *Muzungu* girl.

Hmmm . . . you know what?

A smile crosses his face.

I got the perfect stuff for you. Know that this is only reserved for the best of the best. So be grateful! Welcome to my "secret stash."

Remember how we used to have those toy drinks in small bottles? Your go-to was pink, mine was blue. Blue has always been better, now it comes in adult form.

He grabs a liquor bottle with a bright blue liquid in it.

MAKAMBE: I really do appreciate the thought, but . . .

COUSIN: *(pouring four shots)* Are you so soft that you can't even take a shot at your own party? No more of this. This is your day, you're gonna drink, you're gonna have fun! I won't leave you alone till you do.

MAKAMBE: If I drink I'll get distracted and I won't be able to find him.

COUSIN: Find who? Find *who*?

He hands her the shot. An upbeat Zambian hip hop song begins to play at full volume.

MAKAMBE: This looks interesting. Did you make it yourself?

COUSIN: It's called Zappa. Special stuff made right here in Zambia. Bet you can't get it where you're "from."

MAKAMBE: Is it supposed to glow in the dark?

COUSIN: As you Canadians like to say, YOLO!

COUSIN takes a shot. MAKAMBE takes a shot.

MAKAMBE: That's awful.

COUSIN: Oh! I love this song! Let's hit the dance floor, *Muzungu*!

COUSIN exits dancing, with two full shot glasses. MAKAMBE follows behind. COUSIN starts to dance and tries to pull MAKAMBE in. She tries to resist, but . . .

MAKAMBE: Everyone's dancing! My uncle *(we see his moves)*, my aunts *(we see their moves)*, my little niece *(we see her moves)*, even Kuku *(we see her moves)*, my cousin *(we see his moves)* . . .

MAKAMBE takes a shot.

AND ME!!

We see through her dancing that she is totally wasted. She takes the last shot with no hands, putting her mouth directly on the shot glass.

COUSIN escorts a drunk MAKAMBE to her room.

MAKAMBE: Hey, what are you . . . ? I wanna get back to the party.

COUSIN: Hello no, *Muzungu* girl. You loosened up, that's for sure. But then you took it way too far. I wouldn't have let you have that much but I thought you could handle your liquor.

MAKAMBE: *(slurring)* I can handle my liquor just fine.

COUSIN: Too bad you're leaving so soon.

He looks at her.

MAKAMBE: What?

COUSIN: From that angle, you look like Mum.

MAKAMBE: *(realizing)* That's a compliment.

COUSIN: Why didn't you come to the funeral?

Beat.

MAKAMBE: I had school.

COUSIN: Aren't you supposed to be in school now?

Your mum called yesterday and she said you were writing your exams, so obviously she doesn't know you're here. Is everything okay?

MAKAMBE: Everything is not okay. I need help . . . and focus, to achieve the task at hand . . . What I don't need is family time because I didn't come here for that.

MAKAMBE pushes COUSIN away.

COUSIN: You're cut. Only Panadol and the good Lord can help you now.

COUSIN hands her her PJS.

Go to bed.

MAKAMBE: You can't tell me what to do. You're not Aunty Monje!

COUSIN: I KNOW THAT.

COUSIN, hurt, exits. MAKAMBE drunkenly gets dressed.

MAKAMBE: *(to audience)* How do you find a shadow after sixteen years?

I'll tell you. You lie to your mom, max out your SPC Mastercard on FlightHub, ditch school in the middle of finals, and fly to Lusaka. And then you look for him at a party, but guess what—you don't remember his face or his name, and you can't ask anyone about it because no one understands.

Shit.

Ever since that guy at school threatened me, I have the same dream, every night. I am five? And he's there and I'm lying down and he's crawling all over me. I see his hands, but I never see his face.

He always finds me.

What if tonight I embraced the dream and waited for him—and *made him* show me who he is?

> *Intentionally, she puts herself to sleep, and then wakes up into her dream.*

THE VILLAIN RETURNS

A Movement Piece: The VILLAIN*'s fingers return, but this time it escalates.* MAKAMBE *tries to defend herself.*

MAKAMBE: Who are you? What's your name? Show me your face!

The VILLAIN *takes control of* MAKAMBE*.* MAKAMBE *wakes up, terrified. She exits.*

KUKU *enters.*

As she speaks, she puts clothes into her wash basin, washes them, wrings them out, and then hangs them on the clothesline.

KUKU: *Bananca ni macembele abaswani.* Let me say this in your tongue: The young and the old are so different, you see. Different ways of walking, different ways of talking—different ways of wearing the same shirt. Different. She reminds me of my pupils—from the days when I was known in this town not as a *kuku*, but as one of the very first school teachers. The young ones, they would open up their exercise books and write down everything I said. I watched them listen closely when I spoke of history, and language studies, and maths. You, as the teacher, are the authority on all things academic, but they think that's where it stops. They think you can't know about them—they forget that you were once their age. They don't consider that you may have faced some of the same struggles that they face, that you may know how it feels—and that even though you have aged many years, and you might not know how to use a new kitchen appliance, or a mobile telephone, that you know something that is even more important than any of those things—you know how to know a person. You know how to understand . . . You know how to take care.

KUKU comes across MAKAMBE's white tank top and with a mischievous smile, rips it.

Oops.

She lays it on the bed, exits.

MAKAMBE enters. She starts packing her suitcase.

MAKAMBE: Travel solo to Africa to do what? I'm an idiot. And I never should have come.

Beat.

What the hell happened to my shirt?

KUKU, at that exact moment, steps through the door.

KUKU: Oh my goodness, this is terrible! Totally, totally spoiled.

MAKAMBE: Did you do that?

KUKU: Why would I, your sweet, sweet *kuku,* spoil your beautiful shirt?

MAKAMBE: I don't know because it was fine yesterday. Then you did the laundry and now there's a huge hole in my shirt.

KUKU rips the shirt even more.

KUKU: This is worse than I thought.

KUKU throws the shirt aside.

You know what? It's probably that young niece of yours, hm. Always rifling through your stuff. Don't worry. Kuku will give you some money to go to the market and buy a new shirt.

MAKAMBE: I can't take your money.

KUKU: I insist.

MAKAMBE: I wouldn't even know where to go—

KUKU: I know. And I will tell you. In the middle of the market, there is one special shop and the man there, he sells shirts just like this one, I've seen them myself.

MAKAMBE: Just like this one?

KUKU: Just like this one. *Teeleza hande.** When you walk out of the gate, turn left, go down near Makishi Road, cross the small bridge. Go through the guava trees, around the blue building, and you should see the market. When you get inside, go straight for about five or ten or twenty metres, turn left at the blind woman selling bananas—go straight, and then right at the stand with not the dried fish, but the fresh fish. Are you listening? Not the dried fish, but the fresh. Behind that stand, there will be one, two, three, four, five booths. Go to the fifth booth, the fifth booth only. That's where you will find your shirt.

KUKU gives MAKAMBE the money.

MAKAMBE: Okay.

KUKU: Go on now. And don't forget to be home in time for supper.

* Listen carefully.

TO THE MARKET

A Movement Piece: KUKU *does a brief dance with her chitenge, a blessing, to send* MAKAMBE *off on her way.* MAKAMBE *goes to market, following all the zany directions.*

MAKAMBE: Okay, so, here's a woman selling bananas . . . I hope she's blind. Then straight . . . and then right at the fish, okay . . . and behind . . . *(counting the booths)* one, two, three, four . . .

From behind a piece of fabric.

VILLAIN: Hey! Simamba!

He taps his fingers.

Yeah, you. You're a Simamba, right? I know you. You got that look like the Simambas.

MAKAMBE: Are we related?

VILLAIN: Of course. This face doesn't look familiar?

She studies his face for a moment.

MAKAMBE: Sorry. You'll have to forgive me. It's been a long time.

I'm actually here to buy a shirt.

VILLAIN: I'll give you a shirt.

MAKAMBE: If I've made it this far, then I might as well go to that booth specifically. Just following orders.

VILLAIN: No, no, no. What kind of shirt do you want?

Free of charge.

MAKAMBE: Okay, I just want . . . like a plain white tank top with the lace.

VILLAIN: Hm.

He goes back behind the stall.

One plain white tank top, with the lace. You're visiting from America?

MAKAMBE: Canada. Did you know Aunty Monje?

VILLAIN: May she rest in peace. I used to help her, all the time. You know, fix things around the house, take care of the yard, things like that.

MAKAMBE: Did Aunty Monje use to talk in threes? Like "These roses are nice nice nice." Or "Children, come and eat eat eat." One time my cousin and I got into the cupboard with the baking supplies, it was a whole thing. I just remember, "You're in big big big trouble!"

MAKAMBE laughs.

I forgot about that.

Any luck back there or . . . ?

MAKAMBE peeks behind the stall.

VILLAIN: Just give me a moment . . .

He finds a white shirt.

Ah, here we go. A plain white tank top, with the lace.

He holds it out to MAKAMBE *for a moment too long. She takes it.*

MAKAMBE: This is exactly what I was looking for. Thank you!

(innocently) Your fingers look familiar.

Beat.

MAKAMBE *runs away, shaken.* KUKU *appears from nowhere.*

KUKU: *Mwanaka. Ki nako ya ku ambola. Ki nako ya ku bulela lika kaufela ze mwa pilu ya hao, mwa mubili wa hao.**

Let me say this in your tongue.

Tell Kuku what happened.

MAKAMBE: Last week I was up late studying for my exams. There is this tall guy who lives in my dorm, and he knocked on my door at like one in the morning. I don't know why I even opened the door, but when I did, his pants were down to his ankles.

He walked into my room and he lay on my bed. I kept telling him, "Hey, you're really freaking me out. I super need you to leave." And when I looked into his eyes—they were blank, like there wasn't even a person in there.

He was huge. I was tiny. I froze.

A few minutes later, his roommate comes in and casually says that the tall guy is just drunk, as he takes him out of the room. When they leave, I lock the door behind them, and I tell myself that I'm fine. When the tall guy starts sending me messages on my social media an hour later, I double check that the door is locked, and I tell myself that I am fine. When I hear him banging on the door a few moments after that, saying, "Open the door! Open the door, you stupid bitch! I'm going to rape you and cut your throat," I triple

* My child, it is time to talk. It is time to say all the things that are in your heart, all the things that are in your body.

check that the door is locked. I hide under my duvet and I tell myself that *I am fine, I am fine, I am fine*, but as I wait for him to go away I'm so scared.

The next day, the school doesn't do anything, and the tall guy starts telling people that I tried to seduce him, and that I did all this sex stuff that I've never even done and the people I thought were my friends stopped talking to me.

That look that was in his eyes? I'd seen it before, in this house. I was sitting there. Aunty Monje left a man to watch us one day. He had come over to say hello or drop something off, I don't know, but she had some kind of emergency, and she had to quickly go and run an errand. When Aunty left, this man said to Cousin, "You, go outside," and he told me, "You. Stay." And then he touched me in a bad way. I was always taught: "Don't let anybody touch you there. Don't let anybody touch you there." All I could think about was how I would be in so much trouble because I'd let someone touch me there.

When Aunty came back, I said nothing. I swallowed this secret so deep into my stomach that I swear I forgot . . . until last week, when that guy banged on my door.

After that night, people at school started calling me the most awful things and I hadn't even done anything. What would those people call me if they knew that when I was small, I actually let someone touch me?

So I came all this way, as a grown-up—I'm big now. I came to find this man and to hurt him. But when I found him, when he was standing right in front of me, I felt that same part of me freeze and all of a sudden I felt little in the worst way, and all I could think was that I had to get away.

When am I going to stop feeling little in the worst way? When am I going to stop being so scared?

I . . .

> *KUKU takes MAKAMBE's breath out of her body and spreads it around the room.*

HEALING

KUKU: *Wena, silumba tuwe! Zwa ku mwanake! Unani bana bahabo baba mu babalela, ba ka ku bulaya kuli u kute! Ukaise!*[*]

> *A Movement Piece:* KUKU *casts the energy of the villain out of* MAKAMBE*'s body and calls in the feminine ancestors of their lineage. The space fills with a healing song as* KUKU *performs the ceremony, which is both for the* MAKAMBE *on stage and the* MAKAMBES *in the audience.* KUKU *draws the energies of healing into her chitenge.*

> *She gently puts the chitenge around* MAKAMBE*'s waist.*

Neuska fosa, mwanaka. Uutwile? Akuna ze u fosize.[†] It was not your fault.

> *Magically, the chitenge makes* MAKAMBE *get up on her feet and move her hips. This is incredibly painful, but it is her release. The dance of release grows to include her whole body. The pain subsides and it becomes a dance of joy, of acceptance, of finding ownership of her own sexuality. It becomes rapid. When the dance is over,* MAKAMBE *is free. She can breathe. She sleeps. Safely.*

> *The next morning.* NIECE *enters.*

NIECE: Aunty Makambe!!! WAKE UP WAKE UP WAKE UP GOOD MORNING!

---

* You evil spirit, I curse you! Get away from our child! She has family to protect her now, and this family will kill you if you ever come back!

† You didn't do anything wrong, child. Do you understand? There is nothing you have done wrong.

Rise and shine, sleepyhead!

NIECE wakes MAKAMBE up. She sets up waida.

The other day, I didn't finish teaching you *waida*. It's your turn. You have to sing like this *(clapping the rhythm) "demama de, upside down"* and then you have to do it how I showed you, okay?

Demama de upside down.

MAKAMBE AND NIECE: *Demama debula upside down.*

MAKAMBE plays waida *awesomely. She jumps between and around the ropes, dancing to the familiar song. The memory of this childhood game is satisfying and sweet.*

MAKAMBE: *Fish double fish double*
Upside down
Fish double fish double
Upside down

Dina Mango
Kotapela
Dina Mango
Fya ku sashila

NIECE: Whoa. Are you going back to Canada now?

MAKAMBE: Yes. Yes, I am. But first can I tell you something? Little girl, I think you're great.

NIECE: Okay. BYE!!

NIECE exits at full speed.

MAKAMBE: These five days have flown by.

She takes down the waida.

There are so many things that I hadn't noticed. Like the way the yard looks when it's this early in the morning, and it's half in shade and half in pockets of sunlight. Or that the flower beds are exactly as Aunty Monje left them. Or that if you listen to the chaos of this house—the little one laughing, the pots clanking, the broom sweeping, the footsteps, repeatedly, there is a rhythm to this life. A clarity. I like that.

MAKAMBE finds COUSIN.

Thank you for hosting me. I know that you went out of your way and I really do appreciate it. And I'm sorry for what I said the other night.

I do think of Aunty often. When she died, I felt it, *(indicating her stomach)* here, but it had been so long since I saw you, that I didn't know how to be, in front of you.

Did you tell my mum that I'm here?

COUSIN: I didn't tell her. But you probably should.

You know I gotchu, right?

Did I not have your back in the flour-in-the-cupboard incident of '94? Terrible two!

MAKAMBE: Terrible two. I should say goodbye to Kuku.

COUSIN: Heh?

MAKAMBE: Is she inside?

COUSIN: Who?

MAKAMBE: Kuku

COUSIN: There is no *kuku*.

MAKAMBE: Come on. Hunched over, chitenge in hand, always smiling—Kuku?

MAKAMBE picks up one of the photo albums and points at a photo.

Kuku.

COUSIN: Uh . . . This is our *kuku*'s *kuku. Muzungu* girl. Did you get into my secret stash? I mean I don't mind, but so early in the morning? Damn.

You don't believe me? Check the back of the photograph.

MAKAMBE: Ngela Mwanang'umbi Liayo. Great-great-grandmother. School teacher. Died 1954?

She crosses into the house and sees KUKU holding her chitenge. KUKU does a loving gesture with it. She gives it to MAKAMBE. KUKU disappears before MAKAMBE's eyes. MAKAMBE looks around the room.

Thank you.

She returns to COUSIN with the chitenge draped over her shoulder.

COUSIN: *Muzungu!* I see you there with a little pep in your step! Even wearing a chitenge now.

He licks his finger and then touches it to her arm.

Tssss. Ouch!

I like the swag.

MAKAMBE: Does that mean you're gonna stop calling me *Muzungu* girl?

COUSIN: *Uni siyezi bulutu.* Next time *au ka taha, u to pota hande nde nde nde.**

MAKAMBE nods.

MAKAMBE: I have no idea what you just said.

* I missed you so very much. Next time you visit, you should actually visit me properly.

They laugh.

COUSIN: We got work to do, *Muzungu*!

A warm song fills the space.

MAKAMBE: Shut up.

MAKAMBE observes the space one more time. Suitcase in hand, and chitenge draped over her shoulder, she acknowledges the spirit of KUKU. She inhales. She exits.

The end.

THE EMANCIPATION OF MS. LOVELY

BY NGOZI PAUL

WRITER'S NOTE, 2022

I selected the 2015 SummerWorks version of *The Emancipation of Ms. Lovely* for publication because it is the original, containing all the key elements that have been carried forward in subsequent versions of the show. As I review the script and notes, I am struck by how the timeless aspects of this story continue to unfold. Like Lovely, there are infinite reflections and possibilities.

My continuing gratitude and deepest thanks go to d'bi.young anitafrika for engaging me with the Sorplusi method—which served as something like a midwife to this story—as well as my collaborators L'Oqenz and Waleed Abdulhamid, whose music is essential to the storytelling, and Roger C. Jeffrey, whose movement vocabulary is as much a part of the storytelling as any of the words in the script. My heartfelt thanks goes out to all of them for their contributions.

—Ngozi Paul, 2022

WRITER'S NOTE, 2015

It seems as though every day I plug into, turn on, or see something on some device, I witness some kind of unbelievable injustice. I see myself in Sandra Bland, in Ruth, Blessing, Hana, Ladi, Mary, Gloria, Awa, and 213 of our young girls who are still missing in Nigeria. We are living in peculiar times, but that seems to always be the case. It's hard to make sense of it all. *The Emancipation of Ms. Lovely* is growing up in the middle of these strange times. We are more connected than ever, and in many ways ever further apart. We are all still looking to love and be loved, to experience our humanity.

I first started working on *Emancipation* during a visit to South Africa. I was staying with my good friend d'bi.young while working on a multi-platform piece called *The 1st Time Project*, about women's first sexual experiences from an intergenerational and intercultural perspective. It was d'bi, the gifted and glorious artist, monodramatist, and now our director, who challenged me to delve into my own story before asking women to share their experiences. Being in South Africa, I was also reminded of the story of Sara Baartman, who has become an icon for Black female objectification and hyper-sexualization in the late nineteenth century, whose bones and vagina were put on display in France for nearly two hundred years. The more I learned about her story, the more I was haunted by it. So much so that, in 2013, I returned to South Africa with our choreographer and assistant director, Roger C. Jeffrey, to visit her homeland, learn about her culture, and see her final resting place in the Eastern Cape. On a quest to understand how I learned to love, what I understand about my body, my life, a woman's life, and what a Black woman's life means in the twenty-first century, I was introduced to reflections of myself in the cellular memory of Sara Baartman.

I count it a blessing to be given a voice to speak about love, heartbreak, and transcendence in these perilous and miraculous times. I am deeply grateful to everyone who has come together as a part of this offering. Ms. Lovely is opening me up. Love is opening me. And I am here with you now.

Thank you Grandma, Mommy, Daddy, Sara, Brett, Jiv, Jeannette, L'Oqenz, Waleed, Roger, and d'bi. We play together at SummerWorks 2015. Thank you ancestors and thank you, thank you community. With all my love.

"Today my heart broke," said the seed, "it itched and ached, I was smashed to pieces." "Ahh," said the burning sun, "you were growing, to blossom you have to break."

—Ngozi Paul

The Emancipation of Ms. Lovely was first produced in August 2015 by Ngozika Productions in association with Pandemic Theatre and the SummerWorks Performance Festival.

Written and Performed by Ngozi Paul

Ancestors: Waleed Abdulhamid & L'Oqenz

Director: d'bi.young anitafrika
Assistant Director: Roger C. Jeffrey
Musicians/Composers: Waleed Abdulhamid & L'Oqenz
Choreographer: Roger C. Jeffrey
Costume Design: Jeannette Linton
Lighting Design: Chris Malkowski
Dramaturgy: d'bi.young anitafrika
Stage Manager: Brett Haynes

Assistant Choreographer: Catherine Foster
Producers: Ngozi Paul and Jivesh Parasram

THE CHARACTERS

LOVELY: Lovely is five. Lovely is eight. Lovely is thirteen. Lovely is twenty-one. Lovely is thirty-four. Lovely is—just that. Lovely is infinite. Lovely is in all the ones around her. She creates all the ones around her, and all the ones around her create Ms. Lovely. She is Afro Canadian, African Canadian, first generation Canadian, Black, coloured, Negro, Nubian, Khoikhoi, and—on the other hand—from the land of Kush. She is from another space and time, and yet here she is, now. When we meet Lovely, she is in the here and now, in the 1980s, '90s, 2008, and today.

SARA BAARTMAN: Born to this world in the Eastern Cape. The daughter of a cattle herder, heir to her mother's spirit. Storyteller, dancer, and seer. She is as consuming as a bush fire and as vast as the ocean. A cheetah. An open heart, blood, flesh, and bones. A spirit from another space and time. Sara is the transcendent.

STORYTELLER: Present, in the ever-fleeting now.

GRANDMOTHER: Was born in the Dominican Republic. Raised on di small island. Loves the Lord. Hates men. Is hopeful for the future—and terrified of it. But Jesus is coming, so we must be prepared.

GRANDFATHER: Loves Grandmother. Resents her child and her children. They are not his children, and everybody should know it.

GUY: He comes around in different rib cages. With plenty of bone to spare.

THE DANCE: The different characters have a vocabulary that is also told in movement.

THE MUSIC: Lovely, Sara, and Storyteller all have a vocabulary that is told in sound.

ACT 1

PROLOGUE

View from the back.

We open on a black hole. The stage is pure black, with a black mound on the ground.

In the darkness, a black hole undulates on a large screen. The dark hole begins to swallow itself as the mound on the ground begins to come to life. From underneath, we see a figure begin to move—

This sequence is performed in movement and music.

Music: begins with acoustic sounds.

The mound comes to life. The sounds of the drums and the soundscape surrounds her. This is a sacred space. We prepare the space for the ancestors to join us. SARA THE INFINITE *is coming to life.* LOVELY *is flowering. Moving from ancient rites, born at the gateway of civilization to twenty-first century twerking. Travelling through space and time. All eyes on the rear. We watch as the story is told with the beats of her bottom. Finding us on the riverside of the Gamtoos, as a young* SARA *prepares to leave for Cape Town. The twerking has transformed into a new ritual, one of invitation and respect for the ancestors.*

The STORYTELLER *is coming to life. Drawing energy from the ground. Performing sacred work. Each moment is sacred. Her body is sacred. She moves from the ground as a seed breaking through the earth. The Universe is moving through her body. Calling in the ancestors feverishly. The undulating at times looks familiar. She becomes aware of us. At moments she is young* LOVELY, *adult* LOVELY, *the fire and the ocean, the stars and beyond. The sequence moves in full circle and ends where she began, the seed of an idea coming to life. She is standing on holy ground. Now and always.*

The movement reaches a crescendo, and just as she began, the figure returns under the drape. We transition into the bedroom, where the drape is now a bedsheet.

SCENE 1
JUST BETWEEN US

From under the sheets, GUY *has a final climax.*

We see figures tussle about as they speak post-coital.

GUY: You know we can't tell anybody about this right? I'm in a situation so . . .

LOVELY: Ya for sure. I'm in a situation too. Let's not make this into anything that it's not. Right?

GUY: Right. Exactly. That's what I like about you, Lovely, you're so cool. My wife doesn't understand me like you do. She is so high-maintenance.

Are we cool? I never thought that we would actually do it. Seriously—we can't tell anybody. This is one we'll have to take to the grave.

He laughs . . . then she laughs too.

LOVELY: To the grave, right. I just have to freshen up.

She gets up to go to the bathroom.

SCENE 2
REFLECTION

Inside the bathroom, here and now.

LOVELY *looks into the mirror and reflected back at her is a live reflection of her.*

As she speaks, her reflection moves, bends, and changes.

LOVELY: What are you doing now? What are you doing? You did it. I can't believe you did this. It wasn't even that good. It wasn't even good at all. Who are you? What are you doing?

This scene is recorded live, looped, and will be played back over the course of the play in the next versions of the Reflection scene.

BLACK LOVE

STORYTELLER: I want to love myself. I am ready to be in deep love with myself. I want to experience self-love. Delicate love. Baggage-free love. Love. Pre-slavery love. Emancipated love. Love that was meant for me love. Designed just for me love. Free free love. Love my body love. Simple love. Why can't a Black girl fall in love. Love. Big nose love. Big lips love. Nappy-headed love. Love. Black, Black, Black love. Classic love. Who the fuck said that you invented love? Love. I want to live in the lap of—love. The get up and walk away if it's not working—love. The stay and heal it if it's worth it love. The sometimes contradictory but never hypocritical love kinda love love. Can a Black girl get a happy ending sometime? Love. Equitable love. Fair trade love and dark-skinned love. Chocolate love. Black with no 'sploitation love. Love love love. The gravity love. Cum into my Black hole and be drawn into all there is love love love. A new kind of happily ever after love. Unbounded love. The fullness of me love. The freedom to just be—love. I want to love love love love.

SCENE 3
ONE DAY

LOVELY spins into the bathroom and closes the door behind her. The bathroom reappears. She addresses the audience directly, but she is still speaking to the Mirror.

The Mirror is the screen which sometimes, but not always, shows a direct reflection of LOVELY. Sometimes the mirror distorts her face; other times, it reveals her imagination.

A young LOVELY speaks to herself in the bathroom mirror. She sings and performs a childhood song.

The Music: Jem *theme song from the '80s plays.*

LOVELY dances and sings along to the entire theme song.

LOVELY: You know the ugly duckling? That's me. You think big nose, buck-teeth, black lips—but I am a swan. For sure. You are looking at Cinderella, only—the Black kind. I am Black Cinderella. Cinderella was trapped. So am I. My mom is always working. My dad doesn't even live here. And my grandma is the strictest ever. So, close enough. But look how it turned out for her. The shoe fit, and she got the prince. I will get a prince. Grandma hates boys and doesn't want me to play with them—or anyone. Grandma won't let me go out. Just like Rapunzel. And I don't even have long hair. But I am sure it will grow one day. Even though now it doesn't grow on the sides at all. Whatever. I can use this towel and one day my hair will grow and be as long as Janet Jackson's. How do famous people get their hair to grow like that? For now, I have my mirror, and I can be anything I want in there. Who needs to go out and play when I can play with myself and the million mes becoming anything I want, with a million stories that end in happily ever after.

I can't wait for "one day." Today, not so much.

She smells and cringes.

It stinks in here. Mr. Howard always takes so long in the bathroom. *(sniff)* Why does old people poo smell different than young people poo? I don't think that I will ever get old. At least I will never smell old. Old like mothballs or something dry—ashy skin. Not old, just bigger.

One day I will be beautiful. Look at you. Beautiful. If you look carefully, my face, its perfectly symmetrical. Which is geometry. Anyway, my face is actually perfect. I just have to wait for my nose not to look so big on my small face—same thing with my lips, my eyes are okay though. My sister says my nose is bulbous. Mr. Howard says "You can tie her lips with a rope." He likes to make jokes, but he is so rude. He keeps promising me sheep eggs and I haven't seen one yet. I have no idea what I would do without my magic mirror. I just love it l-o-v-e it so much.

She twirls around. She stands between two mirrors and discovers herself in the reflections for the first time. She is creating multiple reflections of herself.

Hello, hello, Lovely. Lovely. Hello, hello? Hello.

No echo. But there are millions to the infinity of me. See. Me. Meeeeeeeeeee.

Hello me . . . hello. I love seeing you in there. All the mes to infinity. If I lift my arm, does that make them all move? Yes. It does, and my legs and my eyes. See there, that's the smallest me moving in the mirror. I wonder if I just stare at me. If I can make the small mes move without moving. Is there a small world that I can move with my mind?

She stares . . . and stares . . .

It's working.

In excitement, she starts jumping for joy.

Wait, it stopped working.

She stares . . .

I am moving, even though I am standing still. This is magic. This is Lovely magic.

LOVELY begins to play with her reflection, with faces and movement. Until a loud knock at the door interrupts her.

GRANDMOTHER: Love-leee. Lovely.

Come out of di bathroom. Mi sey come out of there. Nah make mi have to call you again, you hear me. Just vexation up my spirit on the di Sabbath. Just run up an' down here inna di place. Any how you a jump roun' in deer a sweat up sweat and tear up you good church clothes dem. If I have to come in there, I am going to give you something to cry about. You see you. Just vexing up my spirit on di Sabbath. I said keep my name out of people's mouth. I tell you. You children is going to cause me to sin in here. They are going to call di police on me when I finish wid you. I sey get—come and get ready fi church!

A musical bridge where echoes of Sabbath morning church and praise soundscape takes us into . . .

SCENE 4
BLACK HOLE

SARA: Don't call me Saartjie
Call me Sara
In fact
Don't call me anything at all
I am the Black Hole
And so you marvel
And fear my greatness
But I will not swallow your fear
I will first swallow myself
And I will stretch myself through space and time

They examined—weighed and placed my brain in a medical jar for study. Cuvier weighed all my organs, cleaning them carefully. But none of them he examined so carefully as the mysteries that he looked to find between my legs. My posterior, my bottom, my arse.

I refused him earlier, but now, spirit free, body cold, he cut, carved, and cantonized my corpse as he wished. But would never unveil the mystery of the beginning of time to him.

They kept my body and skeleton there for nearly two hundred years. Immortalized for posterity, with my contract and baptism papers.

Laughs.

The women of London and France dress themselves with wire and bone to form a behind as fine as mine. *Le faux-cul*, your bustles and padded bottom can only fashion—but never be—what is nature to me.

SCENE 5
GETTING TO THE POINT

When STORYTELLER *speaks, we are in a new time and space. She is here and now.*
She observes, and she feels.

STORYTELLER: I grew up pretending. I learned how to pretend. To run around and tolerate.

To act like what is happening isn't happening. Denial is my reality. I learned how to tell stories to myself to survive and I'm tired.

I am tired. Tired of being a tragedy.

I am tired of swallowing shit and you selling it to me as peanut butter. That's just enough to drive you crazy.

I am tired of being the one who is supposed to stand it all and make a stack of pancakes from my misery.

Sautéed up some greens to go with the heap of doo-doo you told me to make magic out of.

I did it.

It's done.

You can't tell me that Black women were just born angry. I grew up Lovely. But there is a fucking thorn on my flower. Stabbing my side. You can't tell me that Black lives matter now when they never mattered before. Shot down in the streets, being suffocated in my sleep.

I have transformed your oppression into the Gospel and found a way for it to set me free.

I don't want to overcome anymore. I overcame. Wasting time fighting to be human. I just to be what I am.

Said in stillness. Music changes.

Come on. Let's be fair. I'm not talking about a handout. Just an even playing field in this labyrinth. I said I would survive, and I did. I am still here. Now just give me a fucking break. I am getting to the point where I could burn this motherfucker down.

We transition to sounds of church praise and revival.

SCENE 6
MACARONI AND CHURCH

SINGING: *Jesus loves me! This I know, for the Bible tells me so; Little ones to Him belong; They are weak, but He is strong.*

LOVELY: The best thing about church is the food. Macaroni and cheese, mashed potatoes and Jell-O, and chick patties. Delicious. And you get to pick whatever you want.

SINGING: Yes, Jesus loves me. Yes, Jesus loves me . . .

LOVELY: At church they talk and sing about Jesus. He's nice. I think Jesus is the nicest guy. He's God. God is the guy who made us. I like Jesus. Jesus is God's son too. But God doesn't have a wife. But He has a son. I asked my Sabbath school teacher if Mary was God's wife, and she said no. I asked how God could have a son without a wife, and she said because God can do anything. Then I asked if God doesn't want a wife. And then she told me that the devil was making me ask too many questions.

SINGING: Whiter than snow, yes, whiter than snow; Now wash me, and I shall be whiter than snow.

> *LOVELY in the bathtub. Throughout the scene LOVELY undulates. Sound of bathwater running comes in and out as it pours over her head.*

LOVELY: Mommy pleeease. I want Grandma. I want Grandma. I don't like the way you wash my hair. Don't push my head under the tap. I want the cup!

I feel like she is tearing my head off. She is extra mean when she fights with Daddy, which is all the time. Which is now! She is so rough and so rushed.

Dances.

I want Grandma.

Grandma uses a yellow cup to wash my hair. She fills it up—it's never too hot or too cold. Grandma takes time to make sure that I am extra clean.

Stops dancing.

Grandma puts Dettol in the water. She always gives me a good scrub down to make sure my skin doesn't get too Black. But Mommy doesn't even scrub my elbows and is always in a hurry to get somewhere. She's always mad at something. Probably Daddy. Yes, I know it's Daddy.

Dances.

Daddeeeeee. Rescue me. Help.

Stops.

One day she going to drown me and then she'll be sorry. Grandma wraps me in a towel, and she teaches me how to dry my ears and private parts. Like a proper young lady. Grandma knows I have to grow up to be a proper young lady if I am ever going to get a good man to marry me. Mommy never talks about getting a good man to marry me. I think it's because she doesn't like the one she picked.

Dances.

Dad-eeeee. Grand-maaaaa. Help. The pressure is drowning me.

Stops.

This could be it. Ahhhhh wait. Air. It's over. I can't wait until I am old enough to take a shower.

WONDER WOMAN

The Wonder Woman theme song comes in. LOVELY *spins around like Wonder Woman as the song comes in.*

LOVELY: Wonder Woman. I love my "yoogees." They make the most amazing sound when I walk. Clip-clop. My mom is the most beautiful woman in the world. From head to toe. I love her shoes. She has Wonder Woman boots. They are burgundy. Which is like red and purple but not exactly either one. It's a fancy colour. I used to think that my mom was Wonder Woman. Wonder Woman has the boots. So I thought maybe Mommy could be Black Wonder Woman. She is just as pretty, and she works just as much. But Mommy is usually tired, and Wonder Woman doesn't get tired the way Mommy does, so she's not. She just has the boots.

Music fades out.

And she has the matching clutch—which is a bag only you don't hold it you have to clutch it. Like Lois Lane who works for a newspaper and clutches onto Clark Kent. I can't believe that she doesn't know that Clark Kent is actually Superman. I think she doesn't really want to know anyway. I think that is something that girls do when they grow up. They act like they don't know something when they really do. Just like my mom. She acts like she doesn't know that my dad is going to ask her for money, but he does every single time. And she gives it to him every time and every time she acts like she is surprised. That's why I like Wonder Woman. She doesn't pretend. She is always on top of things.

When I grow up, I will have the most amazing shoes.

SCENE 7
GATHERING SPIRIT

SARA: Deliberate was my desire. I would leave this place. I would swallow myself. And with me take my fire and life, all the mysteries they could never unlock from me. I will drown my fire in this poisonous water of life. I have immortal longing in me. I will stretch out over space and time. I saw your face, Mother. Father, I saw you. Camissa, I see you lighting up the Gamtoos river in the spring blossom. James, I see you leaning over my bed. Asking me to drink. Gathering up my spirit. Wild and free. You cannot claim me. In a flash, as soon and as quickly as I had come—I was gone.

SCENE 8
HALLOWEEN DANCE

Paula Abdul's "Straight Up" plays. LOVELY *sings along to the song.*

LOVELY: *(to herself)* Jodie knew that I wanted to go as Paula Abdul, but her mom made her the most amazing Paula Abdul costume, and she takes tap lessons, so who can compete with that?

JODIE: Who are you supposed to be?

LOVELY: *(to* JODIE*)* Obviously, Boy George.

(to herself) I tried telling Grandma that Madonna was singing about church, but then she saw the video, and that put an end to that. Jodie says that Paula Abdul is Black. It seems like everyone who's Black is not as Black as me. How come everybody gets to be Black and no one get to be white?

JODIE: Isn't he like a BOY?

LOVELY: Ya.

JODIE: Ya well what guy is going to want to dance with a boy?

LOVELY: I hope Paul asks me to dance.

Final song plays.

They are playing the last song. Here come the boys.

(to the boys) Are you going to ask me to dance?

Record scratch.

Where are you going?

She watches the boys walk away.

JODIE: Why can't you just be cool?

LOVELY: Be cool?

SCENE 9
REIGN

SARA: And before that, I left London with my freedom, to France. Home was calling, and Caesar promised we would return home in French silks, victorious. Ah France, they loved their rebellions. This man, we insist he is more worthy to reign over us than that one. And with our freedom, we will reign over you all.

The French would not be denied a chance to see me flourish on their canals and banks. Unlike the English, they love to be unabashedly entertained.

> SARA *performs.*

> *Singing and playing an instrument:*

Itbezi Moia moia Moia wah moia moia (repeat four times)

I came off the stage in the highest of spirits, and a new man, Reaux, handed me a piece of paper. He now had my contract. He was now the owner of my freedom. Nothing could calm my fury. Caesar had taken our earnings and left for Cape Town. Would I ever see my homeland?

Reaux offered me *eau-de-vie*, water of life. My heart was broken. I drank to cool the rage inside of me.

SCENE 10
"PAUL WATSON"

Interior school bus. LOVELY *is eleven years old.*

Miami Vice *theme song plays.*

LOVELY: I have the most amazing boyfriend in the world, Paul Watson. The name says it all. He is just that cool. "Watson."

Each time she says something with quotes, she uses air quotes.

He has the cutest *Miami Mice* shirt. It's like *Miami Vice*, but it's mice. The shirt has "two mice on it." So cool. He has the nicest eyes in the world. Sometimes they are green and sometimes they are blue. He is my boyfriend. He is actually my boyfriend. He says that I am a "cool girl," which I totally am.

We have been going out for three months and twenty-seven days. Next week is Valentine's Day and it's going to be so romantic. I think that will be our first kiss. We ride the bus together every morning. We are like Sam and Diane.

LOVELY *sings the opening lines of the* Cheers *theme song.*

You know. We talk about stuff, real stuff. But then when we argue, it's like it doesn't matter because there is a connection. I crushed on him for a long time, and everybody was like "Ya right, Paul is so cute he is never going to go out with you." Everybody said he would go out with Jodie. Because. Well, because she's so pretty. Right. She has big curly blond—dirty blond hair. She can shampoo it herself. And she wears her jacket open in the winter without even getting cold. I get cold. Everybody said that Paul and Jodie would make the perfect couple, but now look. Why do I have to go out with Lamar or Errol just because they are Black? Hello, they both have glasses. I mean "Errol." Plus, he's Jehovah's Witness. He is such a nerd. And I don't want to go out with a nerd just because he's Black. Don't even get me started. Oh, there's Paul.

PAUL: Hi Lovely.

LOVELY: Hi Paul.

PAUL: There is something that I want to talk to you about.

LOVELY: Valentine's Day?

PAUL: Kinda. I been thinking about things you know. I am eleven years old. And we have been going out for a long time, you know. I was talking to Erroll. And—

ERROLL: Go for it, Paul!

LOVELY: Go for what?

PAUL: Well, if I can't say this, it means we are still going out. I want us to be friends, you know, but . . .

They get up and get off the school bus. Sounds of the schoolyard surround them.

LOVELY: Wait a minute. What is happening? This can't really be happening. No warning. Is it because we fought about Sunny and Crocket on the bus yesterday?

ERROLL: Go for it, Paul!

PAUL: I really like you. But I don't know if you are the kind of girl that I should go out with. We are like friends, you know what I mean. We can play touch football together, right. You know, but it's like, sometimes you want like a cheerleader, you know. Like, not a girl like a buddy girl. You know what I mean?

LOVELY: A buddy girl?

(to herself) A buddy girl? I'm your girlfriend. Say something. Please. Just say something, anything, be cool. Whatever you do, be cool. Jodie says always be cool if you want to be cool. Is he dumping me, I should say it first. I wish I could just say it first. But I don't want to break up with him. I really don't. I still like him. I am going to kiss him on Valentine's Day. He is going to be my first real kiss.

Just say it, Paul.

ERROLL: Just say it, Paul.

LOVELY: *(to herself)* Would someone please shut up the Jehovah's Witness!

PAUL: I don't want to go out with you anymore.

LOVELY: *(to herself)* I feel sick. Oh my god, here comes Jodie's school bus. I don't need this.

PAUL: Are we cool?

LOVELY: Ya we're cool.

JODIE emerges from the school bus. Everybody turns to look at her.

PAUL: See the perfect girl would have Jodie's looks and Lovely's personality.

LOVELY runs off crying.

SCENE 11
REFLECTION V2

LOVELY: I have to get out of this place. I have to get out of here yesterday. Before I got here. I either have to walk out of here or jump out of the window.

You just cheated on your boyfriend with a married man. Who are you? Oh god. I don't even recognize you anymore.

During this scene, the recording from the earlier Reflection scene plays. Again, SARA *moves to the mound. Silence.* SARA *is being watched.*

Murmur of the crowd in a different language, likely Dutch, which leads into the crowd of the congregation.

ACT 2

SCENE 1
THE GOSPEL OF COSMO

The sound of the church in worship fills the room.

PREACHER: Glory to God. Hallelujah. I can feel the spirit of the Lord in here today. Can somebody say "hallelujah"? The spirit wants to speak to the heart of someone here today. Someone is feeling weak—the spirit wants to make you strong. Today I know that somebody has turned their back on the Lord. But the Spirit is here to bring you back. To lift you up. You don't have to suffer anymore. Jesus died for your sins.

> LOVELY *begins to drift off to sleep, into a dream sequence, and starts thinking the sermon has turned into the* PREACHER *preaching about what is really in her mind.*

LOVELY: Tips to get your man:
Smile.
Be Fun. Don't be uptight.
Tell your man you want to try his moves tonight.

> LOVELY *tries out some of those moves which transitions into a "happy dance."*

SCENE 2
MONEY, MONEY, MONEY

Singing.

LOVELY: *Friday Night . . . just got paid.*

Two hundred bucks. I'm rich. Sweet. Nothing sweeter than a paycheque. It's Friday night, just got paid. Do you know how many clothes I can buy at Le Château with this? I love making MUN NAE. I'm gonna get me those short shorts just like Vanessa's. My body is better than hers, but she gets all the attention because of her super-short shorts. Chris says he's a leg man. I'm gonna give him leeeegggggs.

She arrives at the teller and addresses her:

Yes, thank you. I would like that in cash please.

Drum responds as the teller.

Five-day hold? So, when will I get the money?

Drum responds as the teller.

I have work tomorrow and I will see Chris at the rec centre. So.

Drum responds as the teller.

No, thank you. Thank you. That's alright.

She starts walking, then stops at Money Mart.

Okay, Money Mart it is, and it's only three bucks on a hun'. Whatever, still have like 190 . . . Admin fee—

She gets the money and counts it as she walks. As she is walking, her walk turns into a stroll around a clothing store.

One hundred and seventy-seven dollars to do what I want— No, you don't need to follow me around. I am a paying customer today— Plus, Alexis got caught shoplifting, and that totally freaked me out anyway. Thought she had that so down pat. "The layers man, the layers." Come on. Anyway. Lady, you can just give it a rest because today I am popping bottles.

CLERK: Can I help you?

LOVELY: Yes, actually, you can help me, thank you. I am looking for hot pants, please.

They are handed to her.

Yes, thank you.

(to herself) YES! Those are the ones. Oh my gosh, they come in red too. I'm going to need those.

(to the CLERK*)* Yes please. Oh, and the babydoll too please.

(to herself) So cute. So hot. All legs please, lots and lots and lots of legs.

She puts them on.

Yes, this is exactly what I need.

Now with a bunch of bags in her hand.

And what happened to the prince when he rescues the princess? She rescues him right back . . .

I just wish I had the rich guy to pay for all of this stuff.

LOVELY arrives at work wearing her short shorts.

Chris is going to love these.

She's dancing around, carrying buckets and washing tables, talking to the customers.

She talks to different customers.

Hello, sir.

Can I get that for you?

Yes, no problem.

(to herself) They are all watching. I am on top of the world now.

BO: Lovely, can I talk to you for a second?

LOVELY: Sure, okay. What can I do?

BO: I am going to have to ask you to change out of those shorts. They are too. Um. Short.

LOVELY: Why?

BO: We can't have you working in shorts that short.

LOVELY: But Vanessa has the exact same shorts on. The exact same.

(to herself) Change? What am I supposed to change into? She has been wearing them to work every day. See. The exact same. And what am I supposed to do when Chris comes by for free soda? He's a leg man. All that came out was:

(to BO) Why?

BO: Sorry kiddo. Hers don't look like that. Yours are um. Too revealing, too distracting. You are going to have to change. They look . . . vulgar. So, you are going to have to change or go home for the afternoon.

SCENE 3
DECLARING MY FREEDOM

Move onto on the podium. She is LOVELY *and* SARA.

SARA: And before that. The most noble of English creatures insisted on bringing me before their courts to ascertain my freedom. I am free. I was born free, so how I come to be anything other?

My answers were not sufficient for them. They feared for my safety. They feared I was being mistreated. They administered the worst of punishments. They declared me free.

I am in a backwards world here. Man can call things true for writing them down. For making their decrees. They can insist on the absolute fact of a thing when nature says otherwise. They revel in debating the obvious and making it law.

And so, with my freedom papers, by a law that I had not written, with my freedom in hand, I was now a slave to their truth and decrees. And their banging sticks and stone hearts made it so. I travelled from place to place with my freedom. But the morality of the courts Dunlop could not bear, so he left my will to his partner, Caesar.

SCENE 4
IN MY HOUSE

Bathroom. LOVELY *is talking to herself in the mirror again.*

LOVELY: Oh, hey Chris. How are you? Nice game. You guys were good. Nice dunk. Oh really? Thanks. Oh, you like these? Thanks. You really you are a leg man. You're such a perv.

DRUM INTERRUPTS!

GRANDMOTHER: *(voice)* Mi sey come out of di bathroom.

LOVELY: Just give me a minute.

GRANDMOTHER: What are you doing in there? I said come out. People have to use the bathroom. Come out now or I am coming in.

LOVELY *emerges from the bathroom and* GRANDMOTHER *cuts her eye after* LOVELY *as she walks past.*

GRANDMOTHER: What is this? You look like a streetwalker. What is that you wearing, you draws? You, where do you think you are going in that? No, my dear, you are not walking out of my house dressed like that. You look like you are trying to pick up something on the street.

LOVELY: Grandma, that's the style.

GRANDMOTHER: That's the style, that is the style. You are not coming out of my house dressed like that.

GRANDFATHER: *(voice)* She gawn get a baby. Just like she mudda and she gran mudda, but tell her no bodda bring it here. Tell just try and stay out on di road where she pick it up.

GRANDMOTHER: No sa, not out of my house dressed like that. I already told your mother. She is too slack with you. I tired tell you walk straight. I did not come to Canada and raise look how many children for you to come up the last one and bring trouble into my house. NO! Jesus give me strength. It is the style of the devil. The path to righteousness is narrow and it does not include the way of the world. As a matter of fact, where do you think you are going? Out? The sun is setting. It's almost Sabbath.

LOVELY: It's 6:38 on Friday night. Mommy said I could go out. It's the finals of the basketball tournament. It's for school.

GRANDMOTHER: It's the Sabbath. And there is no reason for you to be gallivanting on the road dressed like a street walka no. Mi dear. Just try and sit down in here and meditate on the Lord. Think about the glory of God and pray to him to keep you from evil. No bodda start the balling.

LOVELY: . . . but Mommy said—

GRANDMOTHER: I don't care what Mommy said. In my house, you abide by my rules.

SCENE 5
TREE OF KNOWLEDGE

The PREACHER *addresses the audience directly and asks them to actually do the movement.*

PREACHER: Please stand for the reading of the word.

They all stand.

You may be seated.

They all sit.

Please stand for Hymn number 567.

They all stand.

You may be seated.

They all sit.

Please stand for prayer.

They all stand.

You may all be seated.

They all sit.

In the beginning God created heaven and earth and he saw that it was good. And he gave man instruction. And God said, "This is the tree of knowledge. Do not eat from this tree. If you should eat from this tree, you will surely die."

And the devil tempted the woman, saying to the woman that her eyes would be opened. And she ate from the fruit.

Can I get an Amen if you feel like the devil is tempting you today. And the devil tempted the woman.

And for this, God said, "I will greatly multiply thy sorrow in thy conception." Hallelujah!

SCENE 6
REFLECTION V3

LOVELY: No, I don't want anything to eat. I really should jet. I have to work you know.

(to herself) Am I crazy? Am I my mother's daughter? Seriously who are you? I feel sick. Something is broken. I'm just broken.

SCENE 7
THERE IS A RIVER

Humming "Moia Moia." Layered on top of the river sounds of the Gamtoos.

STORYTELLER: There is a river that flows through me. It's life. It courses through my veins. It lifts me up. I don't know how it all happened, but they still gave us enough. They protected me enough so that there is actually a chance. So could see a way out of my inheritance of oppression. I don't remember anything like it was yesterday anymore. All of my memories have a distant feeling to them now. I look at myself and I'm thinking my knees are fat, my thighs are fat, should've worked out more should've done more, and I look at myself every day and think about all the different ways that I hate how I look. And how I have failed at everything and when something good happens, I don't believe it. It's like a lose-lose situation. I don't trust it. I don't trust the good things and I believe that there must be something better than bad. Time is moving faster, or I am getting older. But yesterday feels somewhere different now. I am still here, and I can see what happened somewhere back there or in front me.

SCENE 8
CUNNILINGUS COMPETITION

GUY: You're so different, you know. You're like really different. I don't know, there is something about you girl. And damn, girl, your body is bangin' and that apple bottom is legendary. How old did you say you were?

LOVELY: I didn't.

GUY: So how are old are you. I want to take this to the next level.

LOVELY: I'm a virgin.

GUY: Well, the dry humping is starting to give me blue balls, you know what I'm saying. You feel like you're ready for more, girl. You're like ripe fruit. If you don't pick it on time it falls and it's wasted and you're like some ripe fruit, girl.

LOVELY: Your pants stay on.

GUY: Girl you are wifey material. I want to get closer to you. I'm a man, we have needs you know. I want to take it to the next level you know. Can I take off your underwear?

LOVELY: You can taste it.

GUY: You want me to go down on you? Nah man that's nasty. Mi no bow cat. No man. What you take me for?

LOVELY: All of a sudden you're Jamaican? My girlfriend says that it relaxes you. Maybe that will relax me. And you never know, this could be the night.

He goes down on her.

Ya. Does it taste good? You seem to be enjoying it. Ya, I like it. It's good. No, your pants stay on. Um. Softer. Stick your tongue inside. Ya, stick your tongue in there. Yup, eat it. It's like ripe fruit, right? And you might just get to pick it. Rock the boat. Work the middle. Deeper. Eat it all. You got it now. Drink it. Ya.

She picks up her phone.

GUY: Are you on the phone?

LOVELY: Don't worry. I just have to let my mom know that I'm okay.

Are you almost done? I really should get home.

GUY: Wait a minute, what about me. What about me?

LOVELY: Keep your pants on. I'm not having sex before marriage.

I'm only fifteen. Is that a problem?

SCENE 9
PACK OF MONKEYS

SARA: Before that, I found myself with these curious creatures. I wondered when their curiosity would turn to suspicion.

A large room would not satisfy them—like the riverbank, they always wanted more. And for this, they would pay. A small room wasn't enough until they offered coins for hidden secrets you cannot buy. Where their coins failed them, they took by force.

Like a pack of monkeys, they approached me curiously. They insisted on pressing until rage engulfed me, prompting the gasps that they needed so badly to breathe.

They delighted in my behind. My posterior, bottom. My arse! Six days a week, resting only on the Lord's Day. To give them something to pray about to their priest in their churches.

The more distinguished, the more likely to see the Boer, the barbarian, and the base. And so, I was surrounded by many persons, one man pinched me, one poked me with their cane. Then one lady, always of the highest family and with the finest jewels, would reach, grab, or hold me where she would know better than to touch. I lashed out at them as fiercely as the fire within me. They were most content when I played the crude animal and Dunlop, the cruel master—to feel secure in subduing what cannot be claimed.

SCENE 10
RASTA MAN DON'T NAM NO PORK

A dry, soft batch all-ages party.

LOVELY: Nice party. So are you a Rasta or are your locks more for—

RASTA MAN: You know differently still. I am not a true, true Rasta you know—but I believe that Rasta Man is in your consciousness, you know—

LOVELY: *(to herself)* Okay, so no.

RASTA MAN: I eat chicken and sometimes pork, you know. But my heart is in the music and the lifestyle. And I know that the herb is a blessing from God. It speaks of it in the scripture.

He offers her some weed.

LOVELY: No. No thanks. I've never smoked. But no judgment. I think that it should be legal anyway.

She takes it anyway, unsure of what to do with the joint.

RASTA MAN: You know you are a beautiful Nubian goddess . . . mmmm you are di original woman. A true empress. I love the colour of your skin. You know that di Black woman is the original woman. You overstand? Everything contained inside of you is actually in the blueprint for all of mankind. You see me on a molecular level— The first woman ever found on the planet earth was a Black woman—they discovered her—

LOVELY: *(to herself)* I know that. I've known that for years. Act like you're surprised. Guys like it when they are teaching you something.

(to him) Ohhhh. Okay. Really. That's really deep.

(to herself) Why does that girl keep staring over here, I mean really. Wait a minute. Is she coming over to us? Whatever white girl. You can step any time now. He's not interested.

BLONDIE: I just have to tell you that you are so beautiful. I love your dreads. They are just so amazing. Really. You look like a king.

LOVELY: Can't she see that we are having a conversation here? Go away. Is she wining up on him? Seriously she has no shame. Why is he wining up on her. Did she just kiss him? Be cool. She just kissed him. Wait, he kissed her! I thought I was the original woman here.

> *LOVELY on platform. As she moves further onto the platform, she takes the spliff from the RASTA MAN. The spliff is the iconic Sara Baartman pipe.*

SCENE 11

The HOTTENTOT FLYER *voice-over is recorded in multiple languages and played while* LOVELY *is on the platform.*

HOTTENTOT FLYER: *(voice-over)* With this wonderful living production of nature, the public have a perfect specimen of that most extraordinary tribe of the human race, whose real origin has never yet been ascertained, nor their character. Which has been so differently described by every traveller who has visited those remote regions of the world; and considering the natural morose disposition of those people (who are scarcely ever observed to laugh) she is remarkably mild and affable in her manners. She has had the honour of being visited by their Royal Highnesses the Princess Elizabeth and the Prince regent, several branches of the royal family, the principal nobility of both sexes, and declared by them to be unexceptionally the greatest natural curiosity of the human species ever to be exhibited and well worthy of the attention of the public. Refuting the malicious reports circulated after her arrival in this kingdom but which have long since proved to be groundless. Over her clothing (which is suitable to this climate) she wore all the rude ornaments used by that tribe on gala days.

Admittance one shilling each.

SARA: I wore clothes to appear nude, feathers from Zulu to appear Khoisan, and bone and bead to build and fashion the answers to their mysteries.

All their curious faces were struck silent. Quiet. They stood there in silence watching me. In a flurry of swiftness, Dunlop came from behind the curtain and spun me around. The silence was broken.

Gasp.

They gasped as if being suffocated.

Gasp.

I spun around quickly to imagine what had taken them so. It was I.

ACT 3

SCENE 1
DADDY

We meet LOVELY *trying to roll down a window in a car.*

The window is stuck.

LOVELY: It's hot in here. Too hot. Imagine if we just could press a button and the window could go down by itself. This car is too hot.

On the radio I heard that you need to turn down the window so that your pet can breathe. I could melt. But I can wait. Daddy is going to take me to see *Breakin'*. Just me! Because I got a report card with straight As! Like Daddy always tells me, "You have to work twice as hard to get half as far."

She crawls to the front seat.

I get to sit in the front seat when it's just me and Daddy. Except for when my dad has one of my aunties in the car. I have a lot of aunties. They always need help from my dad. Daddy has very important things to do if we are ever going to get ahead in this life.

My aunties need to get it together. My mommy never asks Daddy for help, because she's got it together. But if we don't hurry, we are going to miss the beginning of the movie.

Daddy told me it would be better not to tell Mommy or Grandma about my aunties or the movie, because I don't have to carry news. Grandma thinks the movies are the devil's playground. And Mommy always gets mad when Daddy is with my aunties because she says they don't need help from my dad. Daddy says Mommy is sucking his life blood.

It's too hot. I might actually die in here. I would die if I missed this movie. I don't care if we don't get popcorn. I put a patty and coco bread in my purse. But I need something to drink.

He's taking too long now. We have to go.

She gets out the car and goes into the apartment.

Daddy, Daddy? We have to go, or we are going to . . .

Daaa—

She turns the corner and sees her father inside another woman!

Daddy? Auntie?

SCENE 2
MUDDY STREETS

Early nineteenth-century Cape Town. During rainy season. The sights and sounds of that season surround us.

SARA: The day Papa rode off, he promised to come back and teach me the next part of the fire song. But after two full cycles, you could not console my tears. He never came back.

When Caesar came with fancy dress and promises of work in the city and reasonable wages—it's easy to ignore unsettling feelings with the promise of adventure on the horizon.

We arrived in the city where the oceans meet, and I was greeted with mud. Wet muddy streets. Full of Xhosa and Trekboers, free and servants. Rich and poor distinguished by judges' papers.

Caesar told me that I must fall in love. "It's time for you to find a husband. You will make a child and be a wet nurse."

"You will find a white mother, sing to her baby, and share your milk."

I heard the drumbeats so deep that even my muddy feet lifted up off the tavern floor. So, this was the feeling of love. I could sing in harmony to this one. He called himself James, a freed slave in the British Army. He offered me his rhythm and I gave him my dance.

With our daughter Camissa, James would take me to London as a freed man—when the outpost rebellion was over. We would dance and play in

London. Camissa took ill. A fever. James blamed my sharing my milk for the illness of our child. She lost. And like that, James was gone. Knowing the absence of love made my search more pronounced, exhausting and endless.

Alexander Dunlop heard my song for my love. He offered me warmth—

ALEX: Come to England.

SARA: —and passage.

ALEX: We'll stow away

SARA: A stranger in my husband's uniform, my British Bushman. Dunlop promised me bass drums. A place vast enough for my fire and my love.

SCENE 3
DELETE

The sun sets and rises on inertia. She stays on her phone and plays Candy Crush during this scene.

LOVELY: Yup, no texts. Don't call him. Don't text him. We had such a connection. We met at a Black Lives Matter rally for godsakes. He said he was going to call me tomorrow . . . four days ago. He said I was talking to his soul. You don't just not call someone who can talk to your soul—

Phone rings.

It's him! Let it ring—

Phone rings again.

Should I do "busy hello" or "sexy hello" or "sleepy hello"?

Or "sexy sleepy" . . .

She picks up the phone.

Hello? *(to herself)* Busy sexy.

Visibly disappointed.

Oh. Hey girl. Why is your number blocked? Nobody wants your number. Ya, I thought you were him. You think I should call him? Why not? Isn't this supposed to be the twenty-first century? Whatever happened to women's rights and equality and all that shit? Steve Harvey's divorced like three times or something. I don't think that we should be taking relationship advice from a comedian talk show host. His Instagram page is private. He should request me first, right? At least. Ya—I hate Facebook. Oh, he's with a girl in one of his profile pics. They look close, but his status says single . . . no, no I can't see any other pics. Privacy settings. Ya. Actually, there are a few people that I really need to delete from my phone. Okay, later girl. Whatever. If a guy doesn't want to call me, I don't want him. Later.

She takes a selfie and examines herself.

Why hasn't he called? Delete.

Her screen reads: delete contact, yes no. She hovers over the delete button.

She clicks contact. She clicks call. Outgoing call rings.

Hey you—I just got home, sorry I didn't call you sooner. I have just been super busy, and I dropped my phone in the um . . . shower . . . I mean while I was cleaning—anyway, blah blah, it got wet, and it's been acting up. So, sorry for not getting back to you sooner. How are you? Oh, sorry—sure, of course you can call me back. Ya. I'm stepping out so—later—and like I said, my phone is acting up so—ya, yes. Right, I will let you go, okay. Okay, I will let you go. Bye.

SCENE 4
CRAZY GUY

LOVELY: I have no idea what I'm doing with this guy. He is either a genius or he's crazy, but the confusion in his eyes is telling me it's more likely that he's crazy. Ew. Oh my god, he's licking my face. Is he actually licking my face? OK?

Giggles.

That tickles . . . mmm. That's nice. Why do guys lick? I don't like it, ever. How did I end up with this guy? A guy comes up to you in a grocery store. Nice enough. Cute enough. Ugh, don't lick my neck. Ask him something, give him something else to do with his mouth. Yuck.

(to him) How does it feel?

(to herself) Hot? Warm? Okay, he's an idiot. Ya. I am having sex with a crazy idiot. I don't think that he's an undercover spy working for the CIA. I think that he is actually a security guard working at Sobeys and he is actually inside me right now. You really need to take a closer look at your life. Oh. That feels pretty good. I have to give it to him: he's got stamina. Argh. Why do they always change the rhythm just when it's getting good? Stay into it. Cum—you don't want this to be a complete waste of time. Focus.

She grabs his ass . . .

(to herself) Ugh, I have some good pussy? No, no—you whisper that in my ear? Oh gosh, please stop licking inside my ear. I am going to have to get this over with.

(to him) Let's turn over. Ya, I like that.

(to herself) This should be over pretty quick now. Got my secret weapon.

GUY *moans . . . the moan is picked up and echoed.*

(to herself) He's not going to last.

(to him) Mmm. Ya, I like that. Ya, that's . . .

GUY *moans even harder and ends with a growl.*

Did you cum? That was nice.

They kiss.

(to herself) I wonder how long I have to stay here before I can leave.

She surveys the apartment.

(to herself) Well, he does have sensor cameras in his apartment, maybe he is a spy . . .

She lights a spliff.

(to herself) No, he's crazy. And you're crazy for sleeping with this guy. I hope my pussy doesn't end up on the Internet.

SCENE 5
BONED

New GUY, *different apartment.*

As LOVELY *speaks, it is as though she is being thumped on the back of the head in a steady but awkward rhythm.*

LOVELY: He says he's ready for something real. But he—just—keeps—pumping. I waited three months for this? Ninety days, I mean wow. And if I had waited until I married this guy. I would have really been in trouble. It's like he's pumping a tire and . . . Wow. Church guys. Hmm? He's nice. Really. But wow, that's a whole lot of sweat. In my eye and pumping. Wow. Wait. He knows that's my head hitting the—I think he's gonna give me a concussion.

(to him) Hang on my head is . . .

(to herself) That's right? My—ooouch, leg cramp. Neck cramp.

Aah, Aah, aah, ugh.

(to herself) not ugh aah good, I mean like.

(to herself) Wait, is he gonna? Amen. Oh wow. He's done? Thank God that's over.

Different GUY. LOVELY *is on her knees giving a blowjob.*

Mmm.

(to herself) This guy is so hot. I love an artist. So intense. He's not the only one that gives good head. Mmmmm. And I play fair. Give and take.

(to him, with mouth full) Just tell me before you cum, okay?

(to herself) Wait, don't just—hang on. You don't need to push my head. I got this—

She removes his hand from her head.

(to herself) Argh, I'm gonna choke.

Whoa don't push my head like—

(to herself) They don't call this a job for nothing. I mean, honestly.

MMMMmmmm

(to herself) . . . read in *Cosmo* humming really stimulates the—

She gags—he starts to cum in her mouth.

She pulls out, but his hand is on her head.

Wait what the—

He cums on her face, in her eye.

It's—my eye. I look like a work of art?

Different GUY.

Okay, just the tip.

(to herself) Oh my god, he feels so good.

(to him) You can wet it a little bit. You want that nice pussy, right? You want some good girl pussy?

(to herself) Make him work for it a little.

(to him) Okay, you can put it in.

(to herself) It's in? Huh? But? He's such a big guy. Okay. Let me just ride this and see.

If I just lift my—no, that doesn't work.

He flips her over.

(to herself) Oooh pulling my hair is not going to help you. This guy is going to pull out my braids.

The neck isn't better. I don't care how hard you pull. I still can't feel—

Honey, my pussy is not big. It's just not.

(to herself) Is he hard? Whoa, my neck. You're choking—my— Fuck he's strong.

Big dirty slut pussy? I—

He needs to take his hands off my neck.

She starts to kick back.

Okay, um . . . I know, I'll—

(to him) Oh, that's a big. You're so strong. Oh, fuck you're a big strong. Ya, that's—

Man groans.

Damn, that guy was a lot of nothing.

THE GUY

LOVELY: This guy. The guy. We get each other. I'm glad we are just friends. Oh, he's beautiful. Oh, he feels so good. He's going so deep. So much easier this way, no complications. Uh, I'm opening. Oh, this guy, opening me. Wow. Okay, so this is happening.

He moans.

GUY: No kissing. No complications. Oh, you feel so good. I can't believe it. Fuck that ass, girl. Shit. Fuck, you got that Black Ass. Lovely. Now that's a fuck buddy. That black. Big. Black. Tight. Black. Fucking. Hole. You're just a— Fuck. You are the best FUCK. PUSSY Fuck. Your ass—fuck. Your hole—fuck! You are the best fuck ever!

LOVELY: What am I? I am nothing. What am I doing? Nothing. Just worthless. Just nothing. Nothing. No one would ever. No one will. Ever want my heart. No one will. Ever want my love. Could ever love me. Am I just empty nothing. Worthless. A gaping. Fuck.

The sun rises and sets on inertia.

There is a pain in my chest. My heart is hurting me more now. My legs are heavy now. But I have to pull them out one by one, heavy as they are. Right leg. I hate my job. Left leg. I hate my life. Stand up. Someone has to pay the rent. Oh shit, the rent. It's already the eighth. Shit. Shit. Shit.

My eyes are burning me. Update status. Want to crawl back into bed. Twelve friends like this.

I want to tear off my skin. I need to lay down and close my eyes again. Sleep until I die. But the sun keeps coming up every morning. I had some ideas once. I am sure I did. Wasn't I going to be something once? Something like happy. Whatever happened to happy?

SCENE 6
BORN FREE

SARA: I came into this world unexpected, untamed and wild.

PAPA: You wanted to rush and see the flames blossom on the aloe trees. So, like the fiery blossoms, you swept into this world, this time, as my wild thing.

SARA: My father told me I was born free. A wild thing. Freedom is my nature. The youngest of seven children, my brothers and sisters know my name. I am my mother's last child. Her last girl, and she gave me her spirit.

SARA: Don't call me Saartjie
Call me Sara
In fact don't call me anything at all
I am the Black Hole
And so you marvel
And fear my greatness
But I will not swallow your fear
I will first swallow myself
And I will stretch my—Self through space and time.

My bones have been scattered across the earth. But I will open the graves up. My blood has been dried up. But I will breathe life into you. I will put my spirit into you. You will live in your own land. Inside yourself. I will break the earth open with my love. My love transcends fear. I will love you, no matter what. Black love. Free Love. Existing in all there is love. Love cannot be reduced. Boundless love that cannot be reduced. My love is time. My love is elemental. My love is the darkness. My love is Black Black Black love.

FINAL REFLECTION

LOVELY: I have to go. I'm not coming back here again. I love you. I love you and I have to go. I don't need anything that you can feed me. My love is enough to be held. My love is enough to hold. My love is enough. My love is the best fuck ever. My love stretches on forever.

EPILOGUE

INFINITY V2

We are inside the small bathroom. Like LOVELY *Infinity she stands in front of a mirror. She stands between two mirrors and discovers herself in the reflections for the first time. She is creating multiple reflections. This time the space takes on an even more magical quality. She is* LOVELY, *now and then. She is spirit and she is the* STORYTELLER.

LOVELY: Hello, hello Lovely. Lovely. Hello, hello? Hello.

But there are millions to infinity of me. See. Me. Me. Meeeeeeeeeeee.

Hello me. . . hello. I love seeing you in there. All the mes to infinity. If I lift my arm does that make them all move? Move the little me with the mind of me.

She stares . . . and stares . . .

Yes, in there anything can happen. I am dancing in there. And I have my own room. I have enough room. I am flying there.

She stares . . .

I am moving even though I am standing still. This is magic. This is Lovely magic.

She closes her eyes and spreads her arms open wide.

I keep going. Like the stars. Just like the stars in the sky. There is no end to me.

Black hole reappears.

THE SENDER

BY CHERYL FOGGO

This is for us.

ACKNOWLEDGEMENTS

I would like to thank Leah-Simone Bowen for her intelligent direction, and Amanda Cordner for her brilliant performance as Cil in the original production of this play.

I would also like to acknowledge Mumbi Tindyebwa Otu and the entire team at Obsidian Theatre Company for creating the unprecedented project that is *21 Black Futures.*

PLAYWRIGHT'S NOTE

In my vision of the future where *The Sender* is set, a global project to eliminate racism and its associated effects has resulted in a world that is peaceful, logical, and sustainable.

The Sender aired on CBC Gem as Season 1, Episode 2 of Obsidian Theatre Company's *21 Black Futures* series, with the following cast and creative team:

Cil: Amanda Cordner
Director: Leah-Simone Bowen

CHARACTERS

Lucille "Cil" Brown, a Black woman

SETTING

An office space in the future

Interior office space. Day.

CIL is seated at her monitor. There is a large, raised red button at her desk, clearly visible.

She stretches, the end of a long work day. A pleasant tone sounds, indicating her System has logged in.

She touches a device in her ear.

CIL: Hey System.

Yep, pretty straightforward. The couple that ran the Rights for Whites website tried to smuggle a bunch of music.

Ya, no doubt.

Other than that, smooth as glass. Oh, except I had one weird glitch a couple hours ago.

Like a power surge or something. Maybe ask maintenance to schedule a scan of my LX tonight.

So just one more for today, right?

Do I have his data?

A sound indicates a file's been uploaded to her monitor. She gives it a quick scan.

Got it. He's Implicit Consent with a Code 3 Complaint.

Go ahead and upsync us. Talk to you later.

A sound indicates System's departure.

Good afternoon, twenty-six-year-old Terrance Knight. This is Transport Room 5.

Mr. Knight, I understand you have lodged a complaint relating to the diagnosis of cataracts in your left eye prior to signing the terms that will enable your transfer to White Supremacist Island.

The Board of Compassionate Exemptions and Extensions has reviewed and denied your complaint.

No.

That has nothing to do with me. Completely different department.

Now I can assure you, cataract surgery is available on White Supremacist Island.

True, the procedure that utilizes the Laserphaco Probe will not be avail . . .

Not negotiable.

If you would . . .

It's . . .

She lifts a hand and raises her voice.

Mr. Knight!

I am authorized to offer advice at my discretion, therefore I will take a moment to point out that your attempt to shout over my communication is a symptom of your chronic interrupting and multi-splaining. This behaviour is even unpopular on White Supremacist Island and there are a lot of quick-tempered people over there. Consider yourself warned.

The Laserphaco Probe is subject to Statute 43.

Residents of White Supremacist Island forfeit all inventions, improvements, and popular entertainments that can be directly linked to Indigenous, Black, or Persons of Colour. The Laserphaco Probe is a patented invention by Patricia Bath, a Black woman.

You'll get the other cataract surgery once you get over there and it'll probably be fine. Plus, look at everything else you're getting! No, I know you haven't signed yet, but just hypothetically.

The luxury high-rise includes built-in gaming wall, ion-factor surround sound, and a dishwasher. Since you're not a voluntary you can't have the three-bedroom, but I'll get you two plus den with a bath and a half. There's an infinity pool and virtual forest sauna on the 22nd floor.

Well sure, there's always fine print.

The elevators are not equipped with the automatic closing doors that include the flexible belt improvement patented by Alexander Miles, a Black man. This does mean there is increased risk of falling down the elevator shaft, so getting up to the pool is . . . Well. The staircases are safe!

The island has a temperate climate. There are jobs. The beaches are . . .

Her station glitches. The lights dim briefly. We hear a powerful rush of water, a whooshing sound. When the lights come back up, a few console lights are flashing.

CIL: *(to herself)* What's happening?

Mr. Knight! Are you still there?

CIL presses her ear device, attempting to summon System 11-14.

System! System 11-14!

What's going on?

She's on her feet now. She repeatedly taps the device in her ear.

System 11-14 this is Cil.

This is Cil in Sending Room 5. Are you there? I'm having an issue!

She presses the ear device again.

CIL: *(confused)* Who is this?

A long beat as she squints at her monitor and strains to hear.

Who?

Brittany who? Bree?

Bree Corbett!?

CIL *drops into her chair, leans forward to get a better look. She taps her ear device again.*

System 11-14 I've been hacked! Subject Terrance Knight's briefing was aborted before he could sign and he's been transported. I'm requesting a retrieval for signature.

Bree shut up! I'm trying to get my . . .

She's still trying to get her System back.

What?

You got his signature? How? What are you . . . ?

I can hardly hear you. My CPU is really unstable. Just a sec.

Okay that's better. Why do you have my transfer's signature and why are you here?! How did you . . .

Terrance Knight is Terry Thane?

Oh my god. Don't tell me you're still seeing Terry Thane.

How did you get him past my System? I'm not supposed to process files of people I know. A name change shouldn't have fooled it.

Wow. You're still as brilliant as ever I see. Stupidest smart person I've ever known.

I didn't recognize him at all. He looks terrible. Okay, give me the signature. Put it up on the Driver Glide and I can scan it to the . . .

She glances at her timer.

But I don't have time! My shift ends in fifteen minutes and if I don't have it in by end of day it doesn't count! Which you well know from when you worked in Tech and Design!

You'll get me two signatures in exchange for a favour? Who's the other signature? Terry was my last file of the day.

What? Why? I thought you still had six months to go in rehab.

She brings up Bree's file.

I've got your file up here and . . . Dang. Terrible.

Out of the ten precepts of Racism Elimination 101 your scores are dismal on three of them.

Precept 2—Defending the words or actions of racists by saying, "I'm sure they didn't mean it that way."

5—Telling a racialized friend about a racist thing someone said behind their back but refusing to name the perp.

7—Expecting your racialized friends to tolerate your racist partner.

Oof, obviously still doing that.

Okay, this is bad but you've got six months to pull up your scores. Do you really want to spend the rest of your life on White Supremacist Island with him?

All right. Well, that's your choice. You know transfer is binding, right?

You can never come back.

What are the perks you're looking for? No promises, but if I can get them for you I will.

You're 100 percent on this? You know that the end of sustainable life over there is outside our jurisdiction?

I don't know, I'm just. I guess I hoped for better, from you and for you.

Bree. Girl.

Remember when Terry was working at Lineco? And Asif got the promotion Terry thought he should have had? Remember how angry he was when he came over to your place? Ya, we were in the middle of a Janelle Monáe dance party.

Anyway, Terry was looking for affirmation and you told him Asif seemed pretty brilliant?

Ya. He punched a hole in the wall. Does he still pull shit like that?

I know it's none of my business.

I'm only saying that just because he's not going to have Brown folks to blame for all his problems over there doesn't mean he's going to stop punching holes in walls.

Shrugs in surrender, looks at her timer.

Okay, we don't have much time, what do you want?

She types out Bree's list.

Uh-huh. Right. What colour?

For how long? Okay, it's yours.

That'll be tough, those options are usually reserved for voluntaries. Although, I guess you're technically a voluntary, even though you hacked my station. Fine, I think I can get that.

What else?

Nope, that I cannot do. Cool Sports Network is not possible.

Because it includes Basketball, Football, Soccer, Track and Field, and all the other sports that are dependent on majority labour of Black or Brown people. Statute 6, you've read the agreement. I can give you Relaxation Romps Network. It's got a bunch of stuff—curling, lawn bowling, darts, poker, it's still got the NHL, for now. That's the best I can do.

Is that everything?

She taps some buttons on her screen, we hear a send sound.

Done.

All right, load those signatures.

We hear a sound and two pages drop into CIL's hands. She reads them.

She looks at Bree.

Very funny, Bree. Signed "What's her name" and "Who's-it."

All right. One down, one to go.

Brace yourself. It doesn't hurt but it's cold and wet.

Just what I said. One down—Terry Thane, also known as Terrance Knight. One to go—Brittany Corbett, also known as. My former friend.

I don't need your signature, you gave verbal consent. Verbal and Implicit are now valid. I mean we always want signatures where possible, but it's not a requirement anymore. Think of signatures like trophies.

No, he really is gone Bree. Permanently.

Dead serious. You're actually the one that hit send when you hacked in, which is unfortunate because I find it deeply satisfying to punt the Terrys.

Stop it. Oh for . . . there's a box of tissues behind you.

I wouldn't even if I could.

Well look at it from my perspective.

A pleasant tone indicates CIL*'s System has checked in.*

Hey System 11-14. No, I'm okay. Thanks for asking. It's fine, don't worry. See you tomorrow.

System tones out. Without skipping a beat, CIL *carries on with what she was saying to Bree.*

No it wasn't. I was genuinely hoping you would choose to go back to rehab. I wanted you to save yourself.

Anyway.

She stands.

I am going to honour all the things you asked for. And I've added a couple more perks. The tire voucher on Terry's truck is upgraded to the really fat ones, and I'll give you some vintage New England Patriots merch from back in the day. Old time's sake.

She pushes the red Send button.

We hear a mighty rush of water and a whooshing sound.

Bye Bree.

End.

CRYBABY

BY KALALE DALTON-LUTALE

NOTE FROM THE PLAYWRIGHT

In the original productions, the stage was bare with only an old school overhead projector. All the images were either archival photographs of mine, or digital collages printed on acetate and manually manipulated by the performer. There were also tears, but I guess that's in the title.

The first draft of *Crybaby* was written with the support of Playwrights' Workshop Montréal's Emerging Creators Unit (ECU) under the direction of Jesse Stong.

Crybaby was first produced for the 2017 Revolution They Wrote Festival in Montreal. It premiered at the Mainline Gallery on March 26 with the following cast and crew:

Crybaby: Kalale Dalton-Lutale
Set/Costume/Projections: Kalale Dalton-Lutale
Director/Dramaturge: Jesse Stong

Crybaby was then presented in conjunction with *Dark Red* by Willow Cioppa by Black Theatre Workshop in 2020. It was presented at MAI in Montreal with the following cast and crew:

Crybaby: Kalale Dalton-Lutale
Set/Costume/Projections: Kalale Dalton-Lutale
Director/Dramaturge: Jesse Stong
Stage Manager: Kelsey Rae

This production was made possible thanks to the support of the TEC grant from the National Theatre School of Canada.

CHARACTERS

Crybaby

ACT 1

CRYBABY

so, true story
before this
I was printing out all these photos
you know
visual aids and shit
to help you understand
'cause I have all these thoughts
about love
('cause I'm in love)

so anyway
I was at Copies 2000
on Parc
printing these photos
right
kinda in a hurry
'cause I'm late
'cause I'm always late
'cause I'm trying to get here
so I'm there right
and then printer jams
and my photo gets stuck
and I'm watching the guy
and he's taking forever
and I'm like, for fuck's sake

so finally
he rips the photo

outta the machine
and I see it
the photo
that screwed up the machine

She holds up a picture that has been misprinted;
it is unclear what is on the photo.

it's this photo of me
and my mother

in the backyard
of the house I grew up in
and I'm sitting in a pink leotard
on her lap

but right when I'm about to leave
I had to ask the guy
not to throw it out
I had to ask the guy
if I could keep it

that one there
in the garbage
that's all damaged
the one that's all ruined and
ugly the one that's all fucked up

HOW TO BE A WOMAN (AT THE YMCA ON PARC)

copy the woman in front of you doing breast stroke
watch her legs jiggle
swim under water
ignore the old man that looks at you, smiling
who "accidentally" touches your feet

in the showers
with the side of your eyes
watch the old Vietnamese women gossip
hork loogies
wash their bathing suits
pour water in the steam room (even though you're not supposed to)
scrub their backs with pink scrubby gloves
stretch and do exercises that seem good for circulation

you should bring flip flops and wear underwear
so they don't see you go commando

It's a different kind of Black girl if she has a Black mom It's a

different kind of Black girl if she has a white mom

I knew something was really wrong when I was on my mother's shoulders at St. Clair West subway station

I just remember this old white couple looking at us, they asked if we needed any help and I knew

The look on their faces was the way people look at a badly broken arm, you know that something is really wrong

But I was stuck on her shoulders, and I just remember thinking, this is just a dream, this is just a dream, wake up this is just a dream

I noticed from photographs I sleep the same way I did as a child

I used to watch Disney movies

when I was really young

like *Pocahontas* and *Mulan*

She sings a phrase of "Reflections" from Mulan.

I feel like when you sing songs out loud like that, as a kid, or when you're at like karaoke, it's cause you sorta want someone to hear you and be like

—holy fuck dawling! you should sing girl! you have an amazing voice—like holy shit get your self an agent! Girl you're gonna go far!

She sings a phrase of "Lucky" by Britney Spears.

At night I used to masturbate to the Britney Spears poster on my wall

As a kid I always hated the McDonald's breakfast menu
the BLT is the only thing I ordered
I also hated the hash browns

I knew it was someone's job at night to bite all the leftover fries into tiny pieces and spit them into moulds to deep-fry in the morning

I cry a lot at really
juvenile things

I used to hate it
like when I was fifteen and
I tried really hard to
be tough
and I like obviously
don't know anything
about that

I am so like a child
that I thought once I
was a teenager I would
magically live in one
those squat Toronto
looking houses with
like carpeting inside

And in my bedroom there would be a boxy twin bed in the middle with a frilly pink quilted cover. And I would have a lame '80s ornate dresser with a big mirror above the drawers. On the dresser would be a jewellery box that looked like a treasure chest with like, a "nice" necklace in it and a fuzzy photo frame with a picture of my boyfriend in it. The dresser would have "rusty" golden handles and a dark wooden "stain" that is actually like linoleum that will eventually peel back. My dad would have gotten it from The Brick with his "new girlfriend." And I would come home from the Catholic school I went to, with my tartan rolled up in my dark blue cardi with the school crest on the heart, throw my bag on the bed and look at myself in the mirror. I imagined lots of curly hair down to my waist and like a headband.

What I realize is that I basically imagined myself as a random Portuguese girl, whose name was probably like Angelina.

~Hail Mary full of grace The Lord is with thee blessed art thou amongst women and blessed is the fruit of thy womb Jesus Holy Mary Mother of God pray for us sinners now and at the hour of our death~

once upon a time there was this little girl
who was not me
who hated cats
specifically orange tabby cats
that leave and move out
even when you pick them up

and pick them up
and pick them up
and pick them up
and bring them back home

just for the little shit to leave again
I'll tell you when the going gets tough
the cat leaves
and all you got is your dear old dad
his pasta
and television

HOW TO BE A WOMAN (AND ALSO A CHILD)

I watch
some other mother
put a quarter in one of the lockers
stuff their shit inside
turn the key
her little girl asked
sort of annoyingly
to hold it

I wanted her
mother

to tell her to fuck off
that she was too young
instead
she said okay
smiled
and pinned the dumb plastic orange knobby key to the little girl's
bathing

suit

"Smooth Operator" by Sade plays.

I remember a lot of my childhood
to jazzy pop sax like a Sade
interlude.

We used to go to this themed buffet
restaurant for our birthdays, my
sister and I.

"Smooth Operator" by Sade fades.

It was in an old train car, I liked
going 'cause I would eat like four
plates and then lie down in the
booth with a fat tummy ache and
wait for my sister to open her
presents.

I use to make cards for her at
daycare.

I would cut out flowers and
teddy bears from the front
of other cards, and glue
them on top and beside one
another, to make a collage.

'Cause like that's how much
I loved her.

The card looked like an
overwhelmingly ugly pastel
tumour,
but I did it cause, it felt
like, you know one card
wasn't enough.

We played Barbies till she
was like thirteen . . .

My stepmom got us Barbies every Christmas for years.

the girls
the girls!
the girls—
the girls?

my girls . . .

My stepmom took us to the theatre and the ballet,
and she would always read to us, *Anne of Green Gables* or that one where they go to war or Gilbert dies.

She would read to us as we walked down Sherbourne
Street and at the cottage on the hot black
rocks sunbathing and skinny dipping with a glass of white wine.

And on Saturdays, in the cabin when it's quiet after lunch, the CBC would tell us that the long dash indicates the time of day @ 1:00 with a beep.

once
my sister put all my clothes on the roof of our cottage
'cause I hid the Game Boy from her
she didn't speak to me for an entire year after that

I cut the leg of my pants off for her
'cause I had ripped one of the belt loops on her pants while we were play fighting

my dad always said
"it's all fun and games till someone gets hurt."

I remember the the moment
we heard it rip
she just looked at me you know
I'm sorry
I'm sorry
I'm sorry
I'm sorry
I'm sorry

please forgive me
I'm sorry
please forgive me
I am bad I am bad I am bad I am bad I am
bad

so I cut the leg
of my pants off
at the thigh
I think
to show her
you know
how sorry I was
you know
that like
I would
cut my leg off for you

ACT 2
TO ALL THE BOYS I EVER LOVED AND MY MOTHERS; EVERY BIRTHDAY I WISH THAT YOU LOVED ME LIKE DRAKE OR BACON

I'm psychic. I should have known when I was six . . .

Like how you can tell the difference between your pillows.

Like that you know fucking someone who brings a watermelon condom to have sex is having sex with someone who doesn't care about you.

When a nigga hold you down you supposed to drown!

Drake loves me more than you.
He's coming to see me.
He walked into my bedroom last night and kissed me goodnight and rubbed my back. I am the girl in every song.
I am the girl with the phat booty.
No one knows we're dating 'cause I have to keep it a secret.
Or the paparazzi would be on my ass and so would RiRi and Nicki Minaj and J.Lo. And have you seen those three?

Will you love me when I am the next rap star?

**"All my thots were on your dick like it was Brandy Melville but you fucked with me so I'll end you now like that whale, Herman Melville
cause you're played out like that Moby, dick on every beach in Thailand or like all the niggas in all the land who play in a Mile-End boy band"**

[Outro]

. . . wuteva I don even like u, ya lame, 'nd your tumblah sucks, 'nd you don't even have that many followers on Instagram.

Would you give interviews about us on CBC on VH1?
Will you embarrass me?

Like when we went to pick out dresses for the Grammys!!

Or on our court-appointed visits to the Playdium or a pottery-making class . . .

She plugs her ears and says "Drake" as many times as it takes.

When I was in Patagonia, I would wake up at six to talk to you.

I would wake up at six for weeks and walk from our shitty staff quarters in the dark to Skype you.

I knew when you mentioned you were going to visit your ex-girlfriend in New York that it was over, because when you hung up I cried. I cried myself to sleep in the hot afternoon in the loft above the kitchen. And later I woke up at six and you told me you had fucked her.

I stood on the deck of the boat I worked on and looked at these mountains, millions of years old, these giant fucking mountains and they told me to leave you, and I didn't listen.

Instead, I hated you and your new light-skinned girlfriend. And I biked past your house when I was drunk. And got jealous when the two of you had an abortion.

We used to do a lot of K in your bedroom, and once I fell asleep with my eyes open. You got all scared and worried about me 'cause you thought I was dead. I liked that, pretending to be dead so you would care about me.

"Swing Low, Sweet Chariot" plays.

HOW TO BE A BROWN GIRL (BLACK GIRL, WHITE GIRL, OR HALFIE)

I would watch those
Church shows
on TV
on Sunday
'cause

I wanted to be Black
I mean close to god
I mean close to my mother
—I mean
God bless the motherless child

How to talk yourself off the ledge cause sisters are doing it for themselves and the rainbow ain't enough and even Lorraine Hansberry hated *A Raisin in the Sun* after she wrote it so what gawdamn hope in hell do I have ammirite sisters

can I get an ayyyyyyyyymen!
can I get a muthafukkin amen!!

"Swing Low, Sweet Chariot" fades.

How many Black girls inna de place
How many Black girls inna de place
Why so few Black girls inna de place

HOW TO BE A FAMOUS BLACK GIRL

That girl in *12 Years a Slave*
That girl in *The Color Purple*
That fat girl in *Precious*
That mother in *Precious*
That baby in *Precious*
That slave in the play where she burns down Montreal and she is hanged
That girl who played Jamie Foxx's wife in *Ray*
That girl who plays Jamie Foxx's wife in that one with Leonardo DiCaprio
That girl who fucks the president on television
That girl who was in *The Color Purple* who went on *The View*
That ex-rapper who's not gay
That girl in *Monster's Ball*
That tragic light-skin in that book where she's passing and she has some white babies with some nigger hater and she jumps out the window
That girl in that video where she dies in jail
That baby girl in that video where she is pulled out of her chair and beaten in class and no one does a damn thing
That one in that play about witches
That girl who's that pop star who got beaten by her boyfriend
That girl who's that pop star that got fucked up on drugs with her boyfriend and then she died and then her daughter died

HOW TO BE A WOMAN (AT THE U OF T AQUATICS CENTRE)

you thought back then
that it was hard to tell
you were wearing
your sister's
pink ballet leotard
but it wasn't

once it got wet
you could see
the line of your vagina
and the black dot of
your belly button

you didn't have a locker
so you had to bring your stuff on to the pool deck
like your dad told you to

CRYBABY

I think about a lot of things like movies, like montages. The scene that introduces my dad in the movie of my life is a shot of him driving.

It begins with voice-over that goes:
“My dad always horked loogies out of car windows”
and then it cuts to him horking in the front seat of
every car we’ve ever had

a dark blue Toyota Camry
a Subaru Forester

our VW hatchback
and in each car
he has all the different kinds of
facial hair he’s had

a handlebar moustache
a goatee
clean shaven

and it then cuts to him clearing
his throat really loudly and hork
ing and rolling down the window
with one of those manual rolly
ones, and then an electric one,
and then another electric one to
add variation

all without looking at me once

and each time
in the Golf
and the Subaru
and the Camry

I wonder how he does it
horking horking horking
and it never comes back and hits him in the

face.

"Suzanne" by Leonard Cohen plays.

this song reminds me of my dad
and driving
by Dundas and Beverley right by the AGO
but really what I imagine is all the side streets
in between
because he would always say

"Did I ever tell you I used to live on Sullivan when
I was at the Ontario College of Art"

he has beautiful eyes
blue eyes
and long wet lashes

his idea of bonding was watching
***The Holy Mountain* in the living room . . .**

in the living room you danced
on his toes

and then watched him hold
your mother

and they picked you up
and held you in between
as they danced

you looked at the big
brown armoire embarrassed
as they kissed

```
that big brown armoire
would eventually get dis
assembled

the only parts left are
the three drawers my dad
holds his CDs in even
though he only really
plays

The Eurythmics
Johnny Cash
and Leonard Cohen
```

"Suzanne" by Leonard Cohen finishes.

when my mother got lost
so did the couch cushions

HOW TO BE A WOMAN (STILL AT THE U OF T AQUATICS CENTRE)

you were small
in the women's change room
vagina level
maybe a bit taller
by yourself

not
looking at dangling boobs
not knowing
if you should

put on your bathing suit
over your underwear
and then
leg by leg
shimmy them off

Once we went to a Raffi concert.
My mom and me and one of my little mixed girlfriends, three Black girls going to a Raffi concert, because that's the kind of woman she was.

The kind of woman who bought a ticket for me and one for a friend.

She sings "Baby Beluga."

HOW TO SAY THAT YOUR MOTHER'S NOT HOME

I need to wear blankets as clothes
I feel like a grown up when I eat by myself
or take out library books
guided meditation always makes me cry

I was also born in a handbag
all women become like their mothers
and that
is their tragedy

mothers are the real trump card,
no one touches dead mothers.

should I get a butterfly tattoo
should I get a butterfly tattoo
like in memorial
a little monarch on my hip

so only people who have sex with me will see it
and before we do it they'll ask
"why did u get that"
and rub their thumbs over it
and I'll tear up a bit and say
I read somewhere
that they are born alone on milkweed

this is a picture of me and my mother
we have the same cheekbones

She shows a picture that is not her and her mother.

more and more my handwriting looks like hers
how do you write like someone you don't even
know?

ACT 3
THINGS THAT WILL NEVER HAPPEN UNLESS I WANT THEM TOO AND THEN I'LL HAVE TO WORK REALLY HARD FOR THEM AND TALK ABOUT MY FEELINGS AND BE A GROWN-UP AND DO A LOT OF WORK

"Sweet Thing" by Van Morrison plays.

It's six o'clock on a Sunday
and the sun feels like it's setting
in all the backyards
in all the alleys.

We've been working since ten
serving breakfast out of the backyard at my parents
place there is only one thing on the menu;

1. The Classic: Fried Egg, Bacon, and
Good Potatoes

There is a couple of us
friends sitting around now

laughing
drinking Mojitos made with the mint
that grows in our garden.

Marigolds grow there too
for my father
"They last all summer," he says.

I sit down across from u at one the white wrought iron tables
something "good" is playing now.

I take off my apron
slip off my shoes
put up my legs
bare feet in your lap.

A couple walks by holding hands to see if we're still open

we all smile
apologetically
and tell them we sold out of everything.

I should read a real poem now
I should probably give you back
your CD

If I am sad I will eat
If I am in love I will cry
I would rather be in bed right now
I like flowers, does that surprise
you?
a mug will still steam even once
the tea's all gone

The photo of Crybaby and her mother sitting in the backyard is projected, the one from the beginning of the show.

I should write you a love poem
but instead I looked up the day you
were born
found your birth chart
to get to know you
to see if we're compatible

End of play.

ACKNOWLEDGEMENTS

My deepest gratitude to Djanet Sears, d'bi.young anitafrika, Makambe K Simamba, Ngozi Paul, Cheryl Foggo, and Kalale Dalton-Lutale for your important work—it is an honour to collect your plays in this anthology. Thanks also to Roberta Barker, Annie Gibson, and Donna-Michelle St. Bernard for believing in this project. And many thanks to the whole team at Playwrights Canada Press, and to everyone who had a hand in making this anthology possible.

ABOUT THE CONTRIBUTORS

d'bi.young anitafrika is a queer, non-binary african xaymacan tkaron:tonian dub poet, monodramatist, and black feminist decolonial scholar. they are committed to embodying liberatory art practices that ritualize acts of emancipation from oppressions inflicted upon the people and the planet. the three-time dora mavor moore award–winning canadian poet of honour, author of twelve plays, seven albums, and four collections of poetry was recently celebrated as a global leader in theatre and performance by arts council england and is the 2021 recipient of the rosemary sadlier freedom fighter award. d'bi.young's phd research investigates how black womxn theatre-makers in kanata cultivate decolonial praxes and pedagogies of transformation through performance. their doctoral thesis further develops the anitafrika method—a black-queer-feminist framework that emerges out of the dub theory of anita stewart (d'bi.young's mothxr). throughout the last twenty-five years, d'bi.young has written poetry, created plays, published books, developed a decolonial framework, and founded black-queer-feminist initiatives such as fiwi aat space, anitafrika dub theatre, spolrusie press, watah theatre, and ubuntu! decolonial arts centre. their commitment to designing and facilitating decolonial artist-mentorship opportunities has facilitated the growth and development of hundreds of artists on turtle island, in the caribbean, in africa, and in europe. most recently d'bi.young appeared in trey anthony's *'da kink in my hair* to sold-out audiences at the bluma appel theatre in tkaron:to. they reprised their roles as stacey-anne and claudette and introduced two new roles as ifreeka and fitzroy. current projects include publishing *dub poetry to dubbin theatre: the collected writings of anita stewart* and *dubbin theatre: the collected plays of d'bi.young anitafrika*, establishing ubuntu! decolonial arts centre in costa rica, where international practitioners participate in artist residencies using the anitafrika method and writing the first monograph on black womxn's theatre in kanata.

Kalale Dalton-Lutale is a Black queer playwright and performer originally from Tkaronto/Toronto. Her work embraces experimentation, mothers, loss, and pop culture. Some of her plays include *Pinky Swear* (Geordie Productions, nominated for a Tom Hendry Award, directed by Mike Payette, 2017), *Crybaby* (presented by Black Theatre Workshop and Playwrights' Workshop Montréal, directed by Jesse Stong, 2019), *I am entitled to rest* (New Words Festival, directed by Murdoch Schon, 2020), and *Habibi's Angels: Commission Impossible* (Talisman, directed by Sophie Gee, 2020). Kalale is a graduate of the National Theatre School of Canada.

Cheryl Foggo is a multiple award-winning playwright, author, and filmmaker, whose work over the past thirty years has focused on the lives of western Canadians of African descent. Recent works include the release of her NFB feature documentary *John Ware Reclaimed*, as well as the thirtieth anniversary edition of her book *Pourin' Down Rain: A Black Woman Claims Her Place in the Canadian West*. Recent journalism can be found on CBC's Black on the Prairies and in *WestWord* magazine. In 2022 and 2023, her plays *Heaven* and *John Ware Reclaimed* were seen in Calgary at Lunchbox Theatre, and in Ottawa at the National Arts Centre and at the Blyth Theatre Festival. She also recently wrapped shooting a short film about northern Saskatchewan's Black history, scheduled to premiere in 2023. Cheryl is the recipient of the Lieutenant Governor of Alberta Outstanding Artist Award; the Doug and Lois Mitchell Outstanding Calgary Artist Award; and the Arts, Media and Entertainment Award from the Calgary Black Chambers, all in 2021. She was inducted into the Alberta Order of Excellence in 2022.

Shauntay Grant is a poet, playwright, interdisciplinary artist, and author who lives and works in Kjipuktuk, Mi'kma'ki (Halifax, Nova Scotia). A former poet laureate for the City of Halifax, she "creates artworks that are engaging and accessible, but also challenging, rigorous, and informed by deep research" (Royal Society of Canada). Her play *The Bridge* (Playwrights Canada Press) premiered at Neptune Theatre's Fountain Hall, a co-production between 2b theatre company and Neptune in association with Obsidian Theatre Company. Set in a rural Black Nova Scotian community, this multi-layered story of a family torn apart by betrayal received eleven Robert Merritt Award nominations, winning four, including Outstanding New Play by a Nova Scotian. Grant's first stage play *Steal Away Home* won the Jury Award for Outstanding Drama at the Atlantic Fringe Festival. Her other plays include *KK* (Boca del Lupo, Red Phone project), *Passing* (Eastern Front Theatre, Micro Digitals project), and the ten-minute monodrama *Beyere* (Obsidian Theatre Company, 21 Black Futures project). An associate professor of creative writing at Dalhousie University, Grant holds professional degrees in creative writing, journalislm, and music. Her theatrical work for young audiences has toured with Neptune Theatre's Tour Company, and her first solo stage play is in development with 2b theatre. Grant is the author of several books for children including *My Fade Is Fresh* (Penguin Random House), *When I Wrap My Hair* (HarperCollins), and *Africville* (Groundwood), which won a Marilyn Baillie Picture Book Award and was a finalist for the Governor General's Literary Award. Her other honours include an Established Artist Recognition Award from Arts Nova Scotia, a Poet of Honour prize from Spoken Word Canada, a Joseph S. Stauffer prize from the Canada Council for the Arts, and Arts Nova Scotia's inaugural Black Artist Recognition Award.

Ngozi Paul is a trailblazing and multifaceted artist. An award-winning actor, writer, director, and producer, her creations have received numerous accolades, including recognition from the Dora Mavor Moore Awards, Spotlight Performance Awards, Canadian Screen Awards, and the Canadian Association of Broadcasters Awards. Ngozi began her career at the Stratford Festival of Canada before co-creating *Lord Have Mercy*, Canada's first Black sitcom. She then went on to co-create the groundbreaking sitcom, *'da Kink in my Hair*, which changed the landscape of Canadian television. In addition to her acting and producing, Ngozi is also an optimistically-minded writer who has created several notable projects, including *The 1st Time Project* and *The Emancipation of Ms. Lovely*. She is the creator of the docu-series *Care for Color*, which explores themes of love, care, and self-knowledge within the African diaspora, as well as the annual FreeUp! Emancipation Day variety specials and FreeUp! Freedom Talks, which create a unique place for conversations on freedom. Through her production company, Emancipation Arts, Ngozi's content has been distributed internationally and has achieved global recognition. She has travelled the world extensively in both her personal and professional capacities, most notably as a global ambassador for Because I'm A Girl and the Stephen Lewis Foundation. Ngozi Paul's commitment to honesty and authenticity in her work inspires a true sense of beauty in all of her offerings.

Djanet Sears is an award-winning playwright and director and has several acting award nominations to her credit for both stage and screen. She is the recipient of the Stratford Festival's 2004 Timothy Findley Award, as well as Canada's highest literary honour for dramatic writing: the 1998 Governor General's Literary Award. She is the playwright and director of the multiple Dora Award–winning production of *Harlem Duet* (Scirocco Drama, 1997), which was workshopped at the Joseph Papp Public Theatre in NYC, where Djanet was the international artist-in-residence in 1996. Her other honours include the 1998 Floyd S. Chalmers Canadian Play Award, the Martin Luther King Jr. Achievement Award, the Harry Jerome Award for Excellence in the Cultural Industries, and a Phenomenal Woman of the Arts Award. Her most recent work for the stage, *The Adventures of a Black Girl in Search of God* (Playwrights Canada Press, 2003), was shortlisted for a 2004 Trillium Book Award and enjoyed a six-month run in the fall/winter of 2003/2004 as part of the Mirvish Productions season. Her other plays include *Afrika Solo, Who Killed Katie Ross*, and *Double Trouble*. Djanet is the driving force behind the AfriCanadian Playwrights' Festival, and a founding member of the Obsidian Theatre Company. She is also the editor of *Testifyin': Contemporary African Canadian Drama, Vols. I & II*, the first anthologies of plays by playwrights of African descent in Canada (Playwrights Canada Press, 2000 & 2003). She is currently an adjunct professor at University College, University of Toronto, where she teaches playwriting.

Makambe K Simamba is an award-winning playwright and actor, whose intention is to be of service through her ability to tell stories. As a playwright, her solo work includes the Dora Mavor Moore Award–winning *Our Fathers, Sons, Lovers and Little Brothers* and *Makambe Speaks*. Other plays include *The Drum Major Instinct (Mwana Mulena)*, commissioned by the Stratford Festival and the Banff Playwright's Lab; *On Which We Gather*, commissioned by Alberta Theatre Projects; *The Passport*, commissioned by Green Thumb Theatre; *The Livestream*, commissioned by Young People's Theatre; and *MUD*, which won the University of Lethbridge Play Right Prize, the Ottawa Little Theatre National Playwriting Competition, the Alberta Playwrights' Network Discovery Prize, and the Uprising National Playwriting Competition. Makambe's works in progress have been supported by companies such as Alberta Theatre Projects, Obsidian Theatre, b current performing arts, Citadel Theatre, Obsidian Theatre, and Workshop West Playwrights' Theatre. Makambe is also passionate about performing. Select stage credits include *The First Stone* (New Harlem Productions), *Serving Elizabeth*

(Thousand Islands Playhouse), *GIANT* (Ghost River Theatre), *Winners and Losers* (Chromatic Theatre), *Bea* (SageTheatre), *inVISIBLE* (Handsome Alice Theatre), and *SIA* (Pyretic Productions). On screen, she can be seen on television shows such as *Star Trek: Strange New Worlds, Titans, True Dating Stories, Grand Army*, and more. Makambe was the 2020/21 Urjo Kareda Artist in Residence at the Tarragon Theatre, and the co-host of Cahoots Theatre's inaugural *Blackstage Pass* podcast, celebrating Black Canadian theatre makers. Makambe is a proud Zambian who is honoured to be a storyteller through the medium of theatre.